"A Valuable Collection Of Neat Books Well Chosen": The Pennsylvania Assembly Library

Barbara E. Deibler,

Rare Books Librarian, Pennsylvania State Library

Publication of

The Society For Political Enquiries

in conjunction with the

Capitol Preservation Committee

1994

©1994 Pennsylvania Capitol Preservation Committee
ISBN 0-9643048-1-3
Photography: Brian Hunt
Design: John P. Wattai
Production: Ruthann Hubbert-Kemper, Kji Kelly, Elana Maynard, and
    Marianne Wokeck
Printing: Sowers Printing Company

Overleaf: Photograph of fine craftsmanship and decorative designs found on the
spines of various published works in the collection. Notice the masonic insignias
present on the third book from the right.

DEDICATED
IN MEMORY OF
BARBARA E. DEIBLER
August 11, 1943-July 12, 1991

This book is dedicated to the memory of Barbara E. Deibler, an individual whose contribution to the Pennsylvania State General Assembly and State Library will never be forgotten. While serving as the Rare Books Librarian at the State Library, Ms. Deibler researched the history of the original library collection of the General Assembly. Through her exhaustive efforts she taught and continues to teach fellow Pennsylvanians about their valued heritage.

While helping to teach and heighten awareness of the General Assembly collection, Ms. Deibler suggested that Members reinstitute a practice of centuries past. It was suggested that Members take their oath of office on the original Assembly Bible used years before. The year was 1981, the 300th Anniversary of the founding of Pennsylvania by William Penn, that the 1739, gold-stamped, "Assembly of Pennsylvania" Bible with its aged leather bindings and metal clasps was placed, thanks to Ms. Deibler, upon the Speaker's lectern in the House Chamber.

One of the first projects recommended by the Capitol Preservation Committee and financed by Legislative Leaders was a fire suppression system for the Rare Books Room of the State Library. At this time steps were taken to reorganize and reshelve the collection for greater accessibility.

Through the generations the Assembly's collection has continued to serve as a valued resource, whether it be for the scholar tracing legal proceedings and historical references, or the bibliophile who simply admires historic and invaluable texts. Through this book the efforts and legacy left by Ms. Barbara E. Deibler will always be remembered by the Commonwealth of Pennsylvania.

Joseph R. Pitts, *President*
The Society For Political Enquiries

Acknowledgements

This publication was made possible through the efforts of many people who valued their friendship with Barbara Deibler. Barbara's spirit of sharing knowledge was felt by everyone that she met. Her friends saw that the publication of this document was a fitting and lasting memorial to the spirit of a cherished and revered individual.

Dear to Barb's heart was the collection of Assembly books and rare Pennsylvania imprints that she researched and catalogued as the Rare Books Librarian at the Pennsylvania State Library. She proudly shared the collection with all who visited. It was with much personal pleasure that she spent researching the General Assembly's collection, and it was this manuscript that remained unpublished at her untimely death.

It was in 1985 that a group of friends convened at City Tavern in Philadelphia to reactivate the Society For Political Enquiries. This Society was originally founded at City Tavern by Benjamin Franklin in 1787. Through this Society, Franklin wanted to emphasize and promote a civic-minded community with extensive knowledge of their newly formed government.

Serving as an officer for the Society, Barbara continued to hold the position of Secretary until her death. It was through this Society and her many friends, that this publication was made possible. Acknowledgements are extended to *all* the members of The Society For Political Enquiries. In particular one Society member, Dr. Marianne Wokeck, who out of love and appreciation for Barbara's accomplishments, spent many hours editing and proofreading the manuscript; to her a debt of appreciation is extended.

Everyone who knew Barbara personally, or who ever visited the Rare Books room at the State Library, and had the pleasure of having her extend a warm welcome and informative tour through the tomes on the shelves, knew how much this collection meant to her. Her spirit and legacy will always be felt by her friends throughout the Commonwealth.

Ruthann Hubbert-Kemper
Secretary/Treasurer
The Society For Political Enquiries

A Note about the Illustrations

The photographs in this publication not only show the antiquity of these books, they also depict the beautiful craftsmanship and attention that was paid in the creation of, and caring for, these priceless works throughout the years.

Although Benjamin Franklin's likeness is reproduced on everything from money to almanacs, this oil painting, executed by artist David Martin in 1767, was reportedly one of Franklin's favorites.

Franklin was so proud of Martin's work that he gave it to the Supreme Executive Council of Pennsylvania for them to hang in the State House in Philadelphia. The painting was left behind when the Capitol was moved from Philadelphia to the Lancaster County Court House in 1799. Franklin's portrait was subsequently passed amongst private owners for many years until the Pennsylvania Academy of Fine Arts in Philadelphia acquired the work. Known as the "thumb portrait", nicknamed for the way Franklin is leaning on his thumb, the work presently is on loan and hangs in a reception room for diplomats in Washington D.C.

Courtesy of the Pennsylvania Academy of the Fine Arts, Philadelphia. Gift of Maria McKean and Phebe Warren Downes through the bequest of their mother, Elizabeth Wharton McKean.

"A VALUABLE COLLECTION OF NEAT BOOKS WELL CHOSEN": THE PENNSYLVANIA ASSEMBLY LIBRARY

That the Pennsylvania Assembly had its own library in the eighteenth century is well known among scholars of that period of Pennsylvania history. Occasional references to book purchases appeared in the Assembly's journals from about the middle of the century onward. What is not so well known is that a large portion of that library is still in the possession of the Commonwealth of Pennsylvania. The Assembly journals are silent on the reasons for creating and building such a library.

Philadelphians of the mid-eighteenth century were generally a literate people. They had an interest in their heritage and those who could afford it accumulated impressive private libraries. Notable among them were the rich libraries of James Logan, Isaac Norris, and Norris's son and Logan's son-in-law Isaac II. Those whose interests in reading were not matched by their wealth could join subscription libraries. The first of these, the Library Company of Philadelphia, was founded in 1731 by Benjamin Franklin and his friends. Their purpose in bringing together a collection of useful books was to erect a library for the advancement of knowledge and literature in Philadelphia.[1] When the Philadelphians discussed politics, economics, or law they did so with a background garnered from such writers as Locke, Coke, Puffendorf, Vattel, Grotius, Burlamaqui, or Montesquieu. In addition, Philadelphians bought books and they borrowed books from libraries and from one another. When questions arose, they consulted their books.

Against this background it is not surprising that on the afternoon of 5 February 1745/6, the Pennsylvania Assembly ordered the Clerk "to send to *England* for the best Edition of the Statues at Large, for the Use of the House, and also for some large Maps (one of North America) to be hung up in the Assembly Room."[2] Being the Province's law-making body the legislators obviously needed a copy of the English laws.

The clerk, Benjamin Franklin, was familiar with the business of ordering books from London. He was a printer, bookseller, and librarian, who frequently ordered books for himself, his shop, and the Library Company. He had established a correspondence with William Strahan, a London printer and bookseller. However, he must not have considered the Assembly's order to be of a very high priority, for it was not until three months later, in May 1746, that he included it in a letter to Strahan:

> ...And to desire you to send me two setts of Popple's Mapps of N. America one bound the other in Sheets they are for our Assembly; they also want the Statutes at large, but as I hear they are risen to an extravagant Price, I would have you send me work what they will cost before you send them....[3]

As an afterthought, Franklin recalled that he was told to order "some large Maps." Popple's qualified as large at eight foot square, but Franklin added a post script to Strahan's letter:

> P.S. I forgot to mention, that there must be some other large Map of the whole World, or of Asia, or Africa, or Europe, of equal Size with Popple's to match it; they being to be hung, one on each side of the Door in the Assembly Room; if none can be had of equal Size, send some Prospects of principal Cities or the like, to be pasted on the sides to make up the Bigness.[4]

Besides geography, aesthetics seemed to be a factor in the selection of the maps.

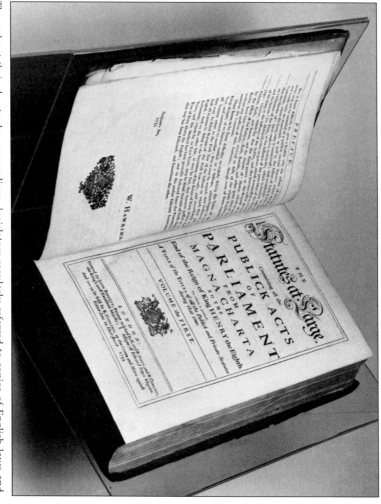

Throughout their day-to-day proceedings, legislators regularly referred to copies of English laws and statutes such as the one shown here. *The Statutes at Large Containing All the Publick [Public] Acts of Parliament From Magna Charta to the End of the Reign of King Henry the Eighth.* (London: Baskett, Nutt, & Gosling, 1734), Vol. 1.

Franklin must have considered the price for the *Statutes* reasonable, for in August 1747 the Loan Office recorded payment of £57.15 to the clerk for the *Statutes at Large* sent for by order of the House.[5] In a November 1747 letter to Strahan, Franklin acknowledged receipt of the books but had to remind his friend to send the maps at his first opportunity. He again suggested that if it was difficult to match the eight foot square size of Popple's, then views of cities and buildings could be pasted together to conform to the size. He also reminded Strahan that they were to be hung in the Assembly Room and Long Gallery in the State House.[6] Finally on 3 September 1748 the Loan Office recorded payment of £77.1.1 to Benjamin Franklin for his expenses as "Clerk of the House, and for Maps, Expenses, and Postage of Letters &c in all".[7] Since several items were lumped together in the reimbursement, it is difficult to know how much of that was spent for maps. At that time the prices of Popple's map ranged from £1.11.6 in sheets to £2.12.6 on rollers, colored. In a 19 October 1748 letter to Strahan, Franklin acknowledged receipt of the maps.[8]

With the seven-volume-set of the *Statutes* and the maps at their disposal,[9] there was no indication that the Assembly had any further plans to establish a library for the use of legislators. There were two subscription libraries in Philadelphia: the Library Company was located in the State House[10] but was apparently only open on Saturdays, and the other was the Union Library Company.[11] Upon his death in 1751, James Logan's rich library was willed to the city of Philadelphia for the "facilitating and advancement of classical learning...," but the library did not open until 1760.[12]

The year 1751 brought some changes at the State House. Benjamin Franklin was seated as an elected representative from the city of Philadelphia at the opening of the new session in October. The Assembly appointed William Franklin to succeed his father as Clerk and elected Isaac Norris II to his second of many terms as Speaker.

On 19 February 1752 the Assembly ordered the Superintendents of the State House to build a Committee Room adjacent to the south-east corner of the building,[13] with access through a door in the east wall of the Assembly Chamber. It was possible that someone had an additional use for that room in mind at the time, because, a few weeks later, on 4 March, the Speaker was requested "to procure for the Use of the House, as many of the Laws of the neighboring Provinces as can be had, and such other suitable Law Books as he may think necessary...."[14] The Trustees of the Loan Office were directed to supply the necessary funds.

As in 1745, reasons were not given in the Assembly's journals for the sudden decision to expand the small reference collection of seven volumes of English statutes to include the laws of the neighboring colonies and anything else Isaac Norris II considered suitable. Norris was also busy increasing his own library. Upon the death of his father Issac, he had inherited an impressive law collection which he added to frequently through purchases from London dealers. His account books in the Historical Society of Pennsylvania's collection and the Library Company of Philadelphia's collection at the Historical Society contain itemized lists of his major private book purchases between 1750/1 and 1757.[15] His involvement in initiating the Assembly's project was only hinted in the journal entry, but is was revealed in a 10 March 1753 letter from Norris to Robert Charles, one of the Assembly's agents in London that it was he who instigated the creation of a library. He told Charles that "the Assembly last year at my request ordered the purchase of a parcel of law books for their use."[16]

Norris wasted no time in placing his order for the law books for the Assembly. There is no record of where or how he obtained the laws of the neighboring colonies, but the "other suitable Law Books" that he thought necessary were ordered in a 16 March 1752 letter addressed to "Thomas Osborne or John Whiston" in London. The letter, delivered to Osborne, included a list of fifty-two law titles, with the prices for almost all the books, and grouped according to size, which was a common library arrangement in the eighteenth century. He indicated that they already had the *Statutes* to the fourteenth year of King George II (1740-41), and requested subsequent volumes.[17] In June he wrote to Richard Partridge, Pennsylvania's other agent in London, enclosing a bill of exchange and adding seven titles that he had forgotten to include in the 16 March letter.[18] By August the Loan Office had reimbursed him £170 toward the purchase of books and window glass.[19] The cost of the books was £70 sterling[20] or about

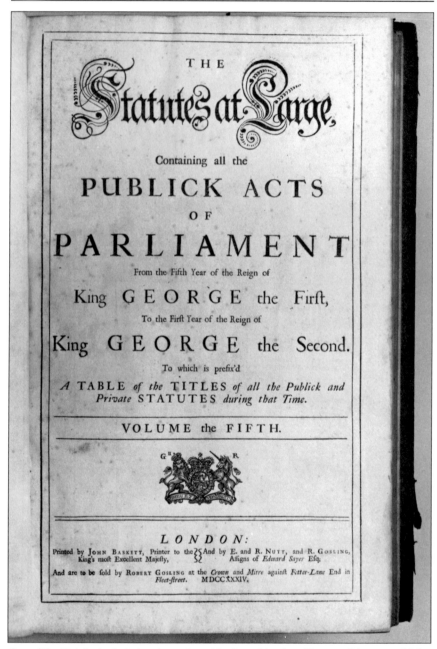

THE

Statutes at Large,

Containing all the

PUBLICK ACTS

OF

PARLIAMENT

From the Fifth Year of the Reign of

King GEORGE the Firft,

To the Firft Year of the Reign of

King GEORGE the Second.

To which is prefix'd

A TABLE *of the* TITLES *of all the Publick and*
Private STATUTES *during that Time.*

VOLUME the FIFTH.

LONDON:

Printed by JOHN BASKETT, Printer to the King's moft Excellent Majefty, And by E. and R. NUTT, and R. GOSLING, Affigns of *Edward Sayer* Efq;

And are to be fold by ROBERT GOSLING at the *Crown* and *Mitre* againft *Fetter-Lane* End in *Fleet-ftreet.* MDCCXXXIV.

One of the *Statutes* included and mentioned by Isaac Norris to Thomas Osborne and John Whiston is shown here. *The Statutes at Large Containing All the Publick [Public] Acts of Parliament From the Fifth Year of the Reign of King George the Firft [First], To the Firft [First] Year of the Reign of the Reign of King George the Second.* (London: Baskett, Nutt, & Gosling), Vol. 5.

£119 in Pennsylvania Currency. The window glass was probably for the new Committee Room.

When the books arrived the members of the Assembly almost immediately set about to enlarge the collection. On 16 January 1753, Norris and Franklin were requested "to procure such Books and Maps as they may think suitable and necessary for the Use of this House..." Again, the Loan Office Trustees were directed to supply them with "such Sums of money as they may require for that Purpose."[21] The members were sufficiently impressed with the idea of having their own library that they issued Norris and Franklin a blank check. Norris, however, set his own limit. The letter which he wrote to Robert Charles on 10 March described the events which surrounded this book purchase:

> ...the House are so well satisfied with the usefulness & conve-
> nience of a good collection of law that they have again this
> year renewed their commission—As I now intend to increase
> the number greatly & make it a compleat Library I desired
> them to join Benj. Franklin with me in this purchase which
> they have done & we both agree to make it a compleat collec-
> tion of the best law books as far as five hundred pounds
> sterl....[22]

In the previous purchase Norris managed to obtain more than fifty titles for about £70 sterling, so a purchase that amounted to £500 sterling would have considerably increased the size of the library.

Unlike the 16 March 1752 order, this 10 March 1753 letter was not dispatched shortly after the Assembly's action. It followed almost two months later. This letter was addressed to Robert Charles, the Assembly's agent in London, rather than to a book-seller. It did not contain a list of specific titles as had the two pre-vious book purchase letters from Norris. He explained that he had begun to"draw out a list" but found it difficult and troublesome since he did not have a catalogue with prices. He indicated that Richard Jackson, a lawyer and correspondent of Franklin's would provide assistance in "choosing the best books & best Editions." Meanwhile, Norris and Franklin would compile a list of the books already in the Assembly's possession for Charles's information. Otherwise, Charles and Jackson were to use their own judgment in the choice of the books. Norris and Franklin planned to write a joint letter to Charles in the near future, which would include any further instructions. He mentioned the new room being "added to the State House & which we desyn for the Committees & our Books is near finished."[23]

Norris did not wait for a reply to the first letter before he wrote another two-and-a-half weeks later. He told Charles that he and Franklin had "agreed upon a joint letter giving directions for our Law Books,"[24] but Richard Jackson could not be expected to provide much help because he was frequently out of London. Therefore, Robert Charles was to bear the responsibility for the selection of the books. As an apology for increasing his work load, but a reminder of the importance of his role in the project, Norris told the agent that "the Assembly will have frequent occasion to handle their Books & I hope thankful for being well served in a thing so continually under their notice."[25] He also included a progress report on the new room—plastering which was about to begin, and glass was expected to arrive in order to finish it in time for the May sitting of the Assembly.

Norris must have been anxious about this project. Another two-and-a-half weeks passed and he sent another letter to Robert Charles. This was virtually the same letter as the previous one: he and Franklin had signed a letter for the law books; Jackson was recently in the countryside and unlikely to provide much help; and a reminder that "the Assembly will have frequent occasion to handle those books & to be well bought & well chosen must make them remember & be thankful to those who have charged themselves with the trouble of the purchase...."[26] He also reported receiving glass for the State House.

In three of Isaac Norris II's personal account books, he entered a transaction dated 1 June 1753 which dealt with the exchange of currency for the purchase of the Assembly's books. In one he noted receipt of £850 for £500 sterling from the Loan Office Trustees.[27] In another he recorded the receipt of £850[28] "to purchase Law Books for the Use of the Assembly."[29] In the third he recorded a transaction with Charles Norris[30] for £500 sterling, remittance to Robert Charles of £850 "to purchase Law Books for the Assembly," and a receipt given to Dr. William Logan for £537.5 sterling.[31] In

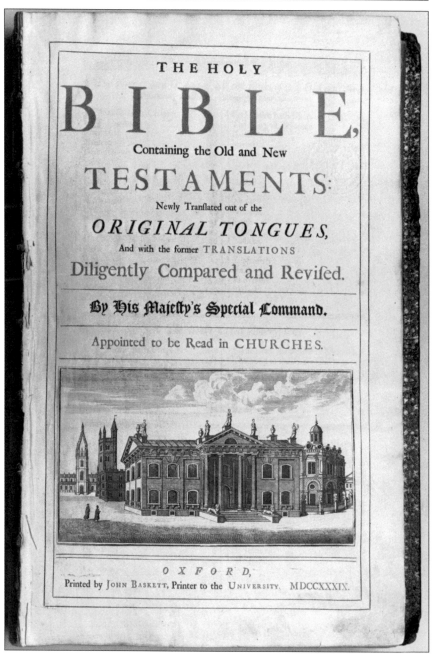

Inside title page of *The Holy Bible, Containing the Old and New Testaments: Newly Tranflated [Translated] Out of the Original Tongues, and With the Former Translations Diligently Compared and Revifed [Revised].* (Oxford: Baskett)

another journal he recorded an August 1753 transaction between Robert Charles and R. William Logan of Bristol, a payment of £537.5 sterling with an advance of seventy per cent or £376.1.6 sterling.[32] Still another account book recorded a duplicate of that entry.[33] An 11 September 1753 entry in the Loan Office Report to the Assembly recorded payment of £850.0.0 cash paid to Isaac Norris "to purchase Books for the Use of the Assembly."[34]

In a 1 March 1754 account book entry, Norris explained the £537.5 error: "I over remitted in my order to Dr. William Logan £37.5.0 sterling. Dr. Logan paid £537.5.0. I received only £500 sterling from the Province—this was paid to Robert Charles for Books &c."[35]

It would appear that Dr. William Logan of Bristol, instead of Richard Jackson, aided in the selection of the books for the Assembly's library. William Logan was a brother of James Logan and an uncle of Isaac Norris II's wife Sarah. In a 14 November 1753 letter to "Uncle," Norris told him that he understood the balance had been paid and the books had been received "which I had ordered to be purchased with that money for the use of our province...."[36] However, the reason for the overpayment was not mentioned. In another of Norris's ledgers, he recorded the "Account of Books with the Province of Pennsylvania. To my order on Dr. Wm. Logan who paid Robt. Charles the ballance of my account £537.5.0. NB. Miller the Bookseller abated £10.-sterling on ye preis of the books."[37] With that entry he listed twelve titles with their prices that totaled £37.7.0.

By November, the books had arrived safely in Philadelphia after weathering a storm at sea off the capes of North America. Norris's next letter to Robert Charles reported that the books "came ashore without any damage." However, he discovered in his inventory of the purchase that one title, "Nelson's *Authority of Sherrifs*" was missing, as were three of the twenty-four volumes of "Parliamentary Debates." After dispensing with those minor matters, Norris told Charles how pleased he was with the overall purchase:

> And till our Assembly meets or I join with B. Franklin in a joint letter I acknowledge your care in choosing & purchasing our books which I believe will prove very satisfactory to our

Photograph of "The Firſt (First) Book of Moses Called Genesis" from *The Holy Bible, Containing the Old and New Testaments: Newly Tranſlated [Translated] Out of the Original Tongues, and With the Former Translations Diligently Compared and Reviſed [Revised].* (Oxford: Baskett).

House as they are a valuable collection of neat books well chosen....[38]

Although they had hoped to have the Library Room ready when the Assembly sat in May, it was not quite ready to receive the books in November.

Norris was careful to include Franklin's name in each letter he wrote to Robert Charles concerning the 1753 book purchase. But it is doubtful whether Franklin was anymore than peripherally involved in the process. Norris and Franklin probably discussed the matter frequently, but it was Norris who did the work. In Franklin's own copy of the *Votes and Proceedings,* which he labeled "B. Franklin's Services in the General Assembly," he noted under the entry for 16 January 1753, "[With] speaker to procure Books and Maps."[39] However, there is nothing in his published papers that would indicate that he had an active role in acquiring books for the Assembly Library. During 1753, when Norris was busy corresponding with Robert Charles concerning the Assembly's books, Franklin wrote a few letters to William Strahan to order books and stationery supplies for the shop.

When the Library and Committee Room was completed sometime early in 1754, Norris himself probably arranged the books in the cases. The Assembly had spent about £1000 of public funds for the books for this library, not to mention the cost of building and furnishing the room. In addition to the major purchases from London which have been recorded there were also the volumes of laws from the neighboring colonies which appear in inventories of the Library but which have no history of purchase. Up until this point rules for the use of this collection had not yet been established. It is doubtful that anyone who was not a member of the Assembly or Provincial Council had access to it. The Assembly Clerk was probably responsible for its care.

A library of this size and importance required more than a clerk to maintain the books on the shelves and ensure that those borrowed were properly returned. Undoubtedly Isaac Norris recognized the need for a librarian—someone with a knowledge of and interest in the books. He must have spoken of this with his brother Charles.

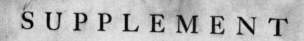

A
SUPPLEMENT

T O

Mr. CHAMBERS's Cyclopædia:

O R,

UNIVERSAL DICTIONARY

O F

ARTS AND SCIENCES.

IN TWO VOLUMES.

VOL. II.

Exeunt Omnes

LONDON:

Printed for W. INNYS and J. RICHARDSON, R. WARE, J. and P. KNAPTON, T. OSBORNE, S. BIRT, T. and T. LONGMAN, D. BROWNE, C. HITCH and L. HAWES, J. HODGES, J. SHUCKBURGH, A. MILLAR, J. and J. RIVINGTON, J. WARD, M. SENEX, and the Executors of J. DARBY.

M. DCC. LIII.

Inside title page from *A Supplement to Mr. Chamber's Cyclopaedia [Cyclopedia]: or, University Dictionary or Arts and Sciences.* (London: Baskett).

Charles Norris was a prominent Philadelphia merchant, bookman, and since 30 January 1750, a Trustee of the General Loan Office.[40] In the latter capacity he was responsible for the office's reimbursing Isaac for the book purchases. He was familiar with the value of the library in terms of resource materials and in pounds sterling. On 26 December 1754 Charles Norris petitioned the Assembly:

> ...setting forth that the Petitioner is informed that some of the Members of this House have lately represented the Necessity of having a Person to take Care of the Library belonging to the Assembly; the Petitioner therefore begs Leave to offer himself for that Service.[41]

After consideration of this matter, the House passed a resolution making Charles Norris "Keeper of the Assembly Library"—the first appointed provincial Librarian. His only charge was to "observe such Directions therein as shall be hereafter given him by this House."[42] There are no records in the Loan Office Reports of any salary paid to him in that capacity.

Nothing more appears in the journals about Charles Norris's tenure as librarian. However, it is evident from references to book titles from the collection that occasionally appeared in the journals, that members used the books in their library. For example, the Assembly noted in their reply to Governor Robert Hunter Morris's message of 13 August 1755, in which he proposed a law to tax the people of Pennsylvania to support the defense of the Proprietary Estate, then exempt the Proprietary Estate from any part of the tax:

> We are not any of us Lawyers by Profession, and would not venture to dispute the Governor's Opinion, if we did not imagine we had good Authority for it: We find in *Viner's* Abridgement, an allowed Book, Title *Descent of Lands*, these Observatins, which we hope may be satisfactory to the Governor in both Points.[43]

Although they were not lawyers, the men of the Assembly were well educated and served by a fine law library and astute librarian.

Andrew Burnaby, an English gentleman, toured the Middle

Colonies including Philadelphia during 1759 and 1760. In his journal he recorded his observations on the State House:

> The stadt-house is a large, handsome, though heavy building; in this are held the councils, the assemblies, and supreme courts; there are apartments in it also for the accommodation of Indian chiefs or sachems; likewise two libraries; one belonging to the province; the other to a society, which was incorporated about ten years ago, and consists of sixty members....[44]

The library occupied the "upper room of the westernmost Office adjoining to the State House"[45] from 1740 until 1773, when it moved to Carpenter's Hall.

Charles Norris died on 15 January 1766. His obituary noted only his service as a Trustee of the Loan Office.[46] Isaac Norris died on 13 July following an illness of over two years.[47] Franklin was in London serving as one of Pennsylvania's agents. By the end of 1766, those who were most closely involved with the birth and early growth of the Assembly Library were gone and the torch was passed to a new generation.

The Assembly Clerk, Charles Moore, was given the responsibility of caring for the library. One of his first assignments was to inventory and identify the books that belonged there. In January 1767 he was ordered to "cause a fair Catalogue to be made out of all the Books belonging to the Assembly Library, and order said Books be stamped with the words *Assembly of Pennsylvania,* in gilt Letters on the outside Cover of each Book...."[48] Samuel Taylor, a Philadelphia bookbinder, was paid £17.14 for binding and lettering books for the House.[49] Moore's catalogue was probably a handwritten list of authors and titles arranged alphabetically in a ledger book.

While Franklin was in London in 1772, he received a letter from a committee of the Library Company requesting a set of the *Journals of the House of Commons.* His reply was reminiscent of his days as a penny-wise Assembly Clerk. He told them that the set was not to be had for under 25 guineas or £25, therefore he did not think it advisable to send them. "Besides they are Books rather to be consulted on Occasion than read, and anyone having such Occasion may find them in the Assembly's Library."[50]

A sample of texts embellished with "Assembly of Pennsylvania" in gilt lettering on the outside cover.

By 1772, the catalogue prepared by Charles Moore in 1767, had either disappeared or had not been kept current with recent acquisitions. When the Assembly convened in October 1772, they immediately appointed a committee "to procure a Catalogue, to be taken of all the Books in the Assembly Library, to number the same, and place them in proper Order."[51] There was a determination among some members to elevate the "valuable collection of neat books well chosen" to a full-fledged library with a classification system and rules for the regulation of its use. In the post-Norris period, the members seemed willing to assume the responsibility for the continuance of the library. When the Assembly convened in October 1770, Speaker Joseph Galloway was requested "to procure a Continuation of the Debates and Votes of the House of Commons, and the Laws and Votes of the several Colonies of Massachusetts, New-York, New-Jersey, Maryland, and Virginia, for the Use of the House."[52] In January 1773 a committee was ordered to draft some rules for "regulating the Use of the Assembly Library."[53] A few days later they presented their "Essay for that Purpose" to the Chair.[54] The following day the House resumed consideration of the report, debated the issue, then tabled it.[55] It was never discussed again and died for lack of action at the close of the session.

A student of Robert Proud's Latin School wrote in the 3 October 1774 issue of his school publication his observations of the Assembly Library following a tour of the State House. It is one of the best descriptions of the physical library to be found.

> ...The Assembly Room is finished in a neat but not an elegant manner. From this room you go through a back door into the Assembly's Library, which is a very elegant apartment. It is ornamented with a Stucco ceiling and Chimney piece. Round this Room are Glass Cases in which the books are deposited. These books consist of all the laws of England made in these later years, and besides these of History and Poetry &c. The Assembly only have recourse to this library. There are also likewise deposited a most beautiful bust in wax of Thomas Penn, Esq. one of the Proprietors of the province which was sent as a present to the Assembly by the Lady Julianna Penn.[56]

In September 1774, as relations between England and her American colonies deteriorated, Philadelphia became the meeting

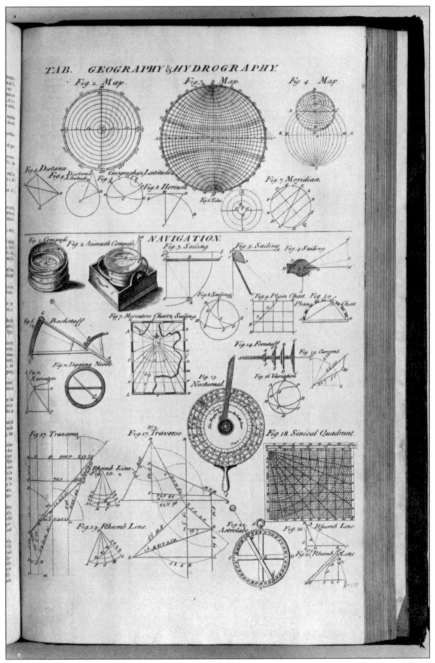

Photograph of "Geography and Hydrography" drawings from *A Supplement to Mr. Chamber's Cyclopaedia [Cyclopedia]: or, Universal Dictionary or Arts and Sciences.* (London: Baskett).

place for delegates from twelve of the colonies. The State House was offered to the Continental Congress for their sessions, but opponents of Assembly Speaker Joseph Galloway feared that his conservatism might unfavorably influence the proceedings. The new Carpenter's Hall, less than two blocks from the State House, was recommended as a more suitable site. The Library Company, a former tenant of the State House, was already occupying space in Carpenter's Hall: that would provide the delegates with access to a library.

When the Second Continental Congress convened in May 1775, Joseph Galloway was no longer Speaker of the Assembly and had requested to be excused from serving as a delegate to the Congress. The State House was used as the site for those meetings. Sessions were held in the Assembly chamber with access to the library through the back door. This was a convenient separate waiting room for George Washington when he was nominated to serve as General of the Continental Forces on the afternoon of 15 June 1775. John Adams recalled in his diary: "Mr. Washington who happened to sit near the Door, as soon as he heard me allude to him, from his Usual Modesty darted into the Library Room."[57] During his absence, he was unanimously elected to the post by the delegates.

The effectiveness of Pennsylvania's Provincial Assembly diminished following the Declaration of Independence in July 1776. The Assembly had been adjourned for the summer on 14 June but when assemblymen attempted to convene on 26 August, a quorum could not be mustered. Repeated attempts failed. Finally on 24 September some business was transacted with twenty-eight members present. On 26 September, twenty-three members met, settled the accounts, then rose in adjournment.

Meanwhile, the Convention of the State of Pennsylvania convened on 15 July and gradually assumed the role of an assembly. Benjamin Franklin was elected president. On 18 July a resolution was passed, giving the Convention "free access to the public library of the state."[58] The Assembly's Library was considered to be public because it has been purchased with public funds; it was not public in the sense that it was open for use by all citizens.

The Convention's purpose to produce a new Constitution

for the state of Pennsylvania was accomplished by early autumn 1776. The new structure was similar to the old; the unicameral Provincial Assembly became the unicameral General Assembly of delegates elected from the counties. A Supreme Executive Council replaced the Provincial Council. The President of the Supreme Executive Council was the state's chief executive officer.

In September 1777, when a British invasion of Philadelphia was anticipated, the Supreme Executive Council ordered the "Books in the Library belonging to the State be sent immediately to Easton in Northampton County & committed to the care of Robert Levers, Esq. of the said county.... Fourteen Boxes & Two Trunks sent by Philip Mosser & Jacob Kuhn accordingly."[59] In addition to the books from the library, the state's papers, account books, money from the Loan Office, and the State House bell were shipped northward from Philadelphia to avoid the British who approached from the West. Some things were transported by wagon, others by boat on the Delaware River.[60] The members of the Assembly, Council, and the Continental Congress fled from the city along the same route. They did not remain in Easton but made their way to Lancaster via Bethlehem and Reading. The state government settled in the Lancaster County Court House but the Continental Congress moved across the Susquehanna River to meet in York.[61]

By 6 October enough members had arrived in Lancaster to conduct the state's business. As they settled into the routine, it was necessary to collect their papers and account books. On 1 October, Assembly Clerk Timothy Matlack wrote Robert Levers in Easton, requesting the papers of his office. However, he indicated that the library books, packed in the rough pine boxes, were not yet needed.[62]

Several weeks later the library books were taken to Lancaster under orders from Council President Thomas Wharton.[63] They had just arrived in Lancaster when Wharton received a letter from Elbridge Gerry, a Massachusetts delegate to the Continental Congress. As a delegate, Gerry requested three titles from the library which were

> much wanted by some Gentlemen of Congress & are not to be procured in this place; if they are to be found in ye

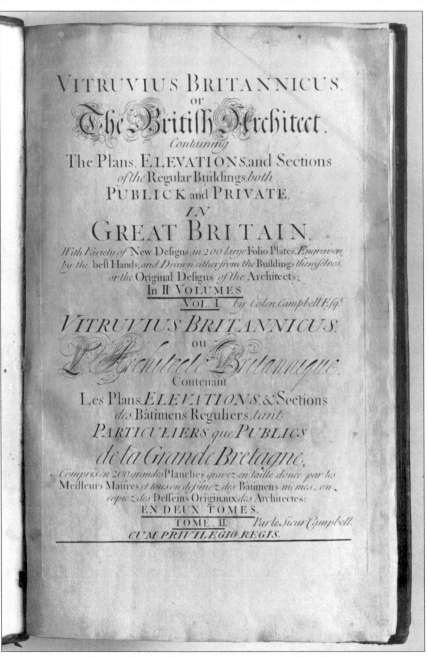

VITRUVIUS BRITANNICUS.
or
The British Architect.
Containing
The Plans. ELEVATIONS.and Sections
of the Regular Buildings *both*
PUBLICK and PRIVATE.
IN
GREAT BRITAIN.
With Variety of New Designs; *in 2 00 large* Folio Plates *Engraven*
by the best Hands; *and Drawn either from the* Buildings *themselves,*
or the Original Designs *of the* Architects;
In II VOLUMES
VOL. I. *by Colen Campbell Esq.*

VITRUVIUS BRITANNICUS.
ou
L'Architect Britannique.
Contenant
Les Plans. ELEVATIONS. & Sections
des Bâtimens Reguliers, *tant*
PARTICULIERS *que* PUBLICS
de la Grande Bretagne.
Compris en 200 grandes Planches *gravez en taille douce par les*
Meilleurs Maitres *et tous on desinez des* Bâtimens *memes, ou*
copiez des Desseins Originaux *des* Architectes:
EN DEUX TOMES.
TOME. II. *Par le Sieur Campbell.*
CUM PRIVILEGIO REGIS.

Inside title page of *The Britith [British] Architect, Containing The Plans, Elevations, and Sections of the Regular Buildings both Publick [Public] and Private in Great Britain,* written by Colen Campbell.

Pennsylvania Library, which we are informed is removed by order of your Excellency to Lancaster, I shall be much obliged to you for ye loan thereof.[64]

The titles requested were "Vattell's *Law of Nations*, Grotius, and Pufendorf."

> Congress must have had an urgent need for those three titles. Not only had they tracked down the library, but they also prevailed upon Pennsylvania delegate Daniel Roberdeau to follow up on Gerry's letter two days later with another plea to Thomas Wharton. He wrote:

> A Committee of Congress have occasion of the under mentioned Law Books, which one of them sais [sic] were in the Library belonging to the State in Philada., therefore I am desired to apply to you for the immediate Loan of them, and that they may be sent by express, if a good opportunity does not very soon offer. If the books of the State were not brought to Lancaster you are requested to borrow these books of some Gentleman there and forward them.[65]

This letter was delivered to President Wharton by either John or Samuel Adams, both of whom had taken a leave of absence from Congress on 7 November and departed for Boston by way of Lancaster on 11 November.[66]

From these letters we learn that the members of Congress had been granted access to the State Library while they met at the State House. The state government was pleased to further oblige the Congress by sending the requested books and paying £9.6.6 to William Irwin for conveying them to York.[67] Congress was satisfied with the prompt and efficient service. A 14 November 1777 letter from Roberdeau to Matlack expressed their gratitude:

> I thank you for your punctuality and care and acknowledge the receipt of the Books five in number, of which care shall be taken. You mention nothing of any agreement with the express, or whether paid or not, he charges 2 days at six Dollars/day, it may be right, although very high, for these reasons I take the liberty to refer the matter to you and beg you will pay the Bearer, which shall be reimbursed on the first Notice....[68]

An architectural rendering of Blenheim Castle found in *Vitruvius Britannicus or The Britiſh [British] Architect Containing The Plans Elevations and Sections of the Regular Buildings Both Publick [Public] and Private in Great Britain*, written by Colen Campbell.

When the Clerk opened the pine boxes to retrieve the requested volumes, he made a grim discovery and immediately informed the Assembly "that some of the books belonging to the state-library which has been brought to this town, were thought to be damaged, by the weather and lying long in damp places...."[69] That probably meant that some of the book covers were warped and that mold had formed on some of the leather bindings. The Clerk had the task of cleaning them and finding suitable quarters to house them in the Lancaster County Court House.

After the British left Philadelphia in 1778, the state government returned and found the interior of their State House in shambles. On 25 November the Assembly appointed a committee to prepare a suitable apartment for a Committee Room and Library and to collect the books belonging to the Assembly Library and deposit them in the new quarters.[70] The State Treasurer's accounts indicated that more than £140 was spent on lumber and carpentry work for the new room by early 1779.[71] These accounts also indicated that John Jacobs was paid £60 in April 1779 "for securing and bringing to Philadelphia, books belonging to the state library."[72]

The new Committee Room and Library was located on the second floor of the State House rather than the first where it had been prior to the move to Lancaster. When the books were finally unpacked and placed on the shelves, it was discovered that many volumes were missing. The Supreme Executive Council directed the following notice be circulated and placed in the local newspapers:

> WHEREAS, divers books belonging to the State Library are missing, & there is reason to apprehend that the same are in the hands of persons who have had recourse to the said Library, & who have neglected to return them; therefore,
>
> Ordered, That Public notice be given to all persons having Books belonging to the State, to return the same to the Secretary without delay, otherwise Council will be induced to think they are detained from improper motives, and to take further measures for recovery of them.[73]

A day later the Council minutes recorded the return by Mr. Drayton[74] of "2 Vols. of State tracts belonging to the State

Library."[75] A week later the same notice appeared in *The Pennsylvania Gazette.*[76]

There was no mention of the number of missing volumes when the library was returned to the State House, nor was there an indication whether anyone in addition to Mr. Drayton returned books. During 1779 and 1780 the Council and Assembly worked to restore the State House and the library. In December 1780 the Marquis de Chastellux visited Philadelphia on his American tour. He recorded his impressions of the library:

> ...I was then conducted into the secretary's hall, which has nothing remarkable but the manner in which it is furnished; the colors taken from the enemy serve by way of tapestry. From thence you pass to the library, which is pretty large, but far from being filled; the few books it is composed of, appear to be well chosen.[77]

The Marquis stirred controversy wherever he went on that tour. His opinions were considered harsh, but in this case they were probably accurate. Renovations were still under way in December 1780 when the Marquis visited. Later that month Council's minutes noted that Thomas Novell [sic][78] received £20 State money, for purchasing materials for inclosing the Library."[79]

Books that were borrowed from the library and not returned continued to be a cause of concern for the Council. In 1781 they again advertised in the local newspapers:

> WHEREAS, the valuable Library belonging to the state has been scattered by many gentlemen having taken Books to their own houses and lodgings which they have neglected to return. And a suitable repository for the said books being now prepared at the public charge, it is MOST EARNESTLY REQUESTED, that all persons possessed of said books, which are well known by the words "Assembly of Pennsylvania" being stamped on the outside, will send them to the Council Chamber, or by a note, inform the Clerk of the Council where the Books are and a Messenger will call for them. As most of the Books composing the Library are very valuable, and particularly useful to the Council, Assembly, and other publick bodies, it is hoped that after this notice no gentleman will retain them.[80]

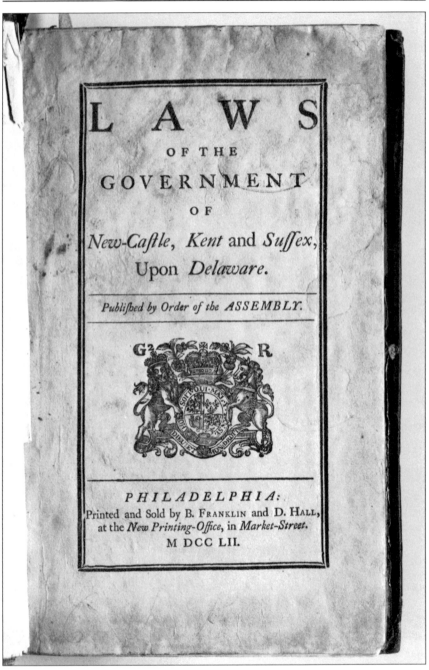

Laws of the Government of New-Castle, Kent and Sussex, Upon Delaware. (Philadelphia: Franklin and Hall).

There is no indication of the success or failure of the advertisement to procure response.

In 1783 the Council granted access to the library to the Court of Appeals in Maritime Cases.[81] In 1784 the Assembly passed a resolution granting permission to the United States Congress, during the time they made Philadelphia their residence, to use the property of the Commonwealth that had been "heretofore used and occupied by Congress."[82]

In 1786, the Council ordered its Secretary to purchase several titles including Jacob's *Law Dictionary* and Vattel's *Law of Nations* two important and missing titles.[83] Jacob's had been one of the titles ordered by Isaac Norris II in 1752 and Vattel's was one of the titles loaned to Congress at York in 1777. Was Congress remiss in returning it?

During the summer of 1787 the Pennsylvania government shared its State House with the delegates to the Constitutional Convention. The Assembly was in recess and the federal Congress had moved to New York. The Council continued to meet almost daily in their second floor chamber with President Benjamin Franklin often presiding. Although no formal action seems to have been taken, it is assumed that permission to use the library as well as the other State House facilities was granted to the Convention as it has been to the Congress.

The federal Constitution adopted by Pennsylvania in December 1787 necessitated another state constitution. By 1790 a new government was in place in the Commonwealth. The unicameral legislature was replaced by a bicameral structure with the creation of the Senate. The Supreme Executive Council was replaced by an elected Governor and an executive branch.

It became the business of the House and Senate to care for a library. Bills to establish a structure to maintain it were introduced and passed in one house but encountered opposition and died in the other. Meanwhile, dissatisfaction with Philadelphia as the state capital grew as the population shifted westward. Finally, in 1799 the Pennsylvania government packed its books and other belongings and moved once again to Lancaster. The Lancaster County Court House became the temporary Capitol for thirteen years.

Photograph of inside pages of a volume of statues and laws. Upper left law, "Cap. V" reads "It shall be felony to cut out the tongue, or pull out the eyes of the King's liege people."

The final decision to make Harrisburg the permanent state capital was made on 21 February 1810. The move took place in 1812. In Harrisburg, the General Assembly settled temporarily in the new Dauphin County Court House until the Capitol was completed in 1821, and the move was accomplished in January 1822.

In the meantime, attention turned once more to the matter of the library. From the beginning it has been a collection of books for the use of the government. There were no established rules governing its use and no bureaucratic structure administering it. All that changed on 28 February 1816 when Governor Simon Snyder signed the "Act to provide for the better preservation and increase of the library." The State Library became an agency of the state government. It was given a legal standing with provision for its maintenance and increase. The Act of 1816 provided for a joint committee to combine the libraries that had been informally established in the House of Representatives and the Senate with the already established joint Library to form a single library and made that committee responsible for all purchases; to employ a librarian—to be appointed annually—at $2.00 per day; and to make all rules and regulations regarding the establishment of a single library. An appropriation of $400 was made to cover the expenses of establishing the Library and it also established an annual appropriation of $600 to meet the expenses.

Today the State Library of Pennsylvania contains over three million books, periodicals, documents, and microforms, but its core remains the Assembly Collection. Approximately two hundred titles, including the seven volume set of *Statues at Large* have been identified as belonging to that original library. The books are located in the State Library's Rare Book Room and most still bear the gilt "Assembly of Pennsylvania" stamp. They are a tribute to an Assembly that recognized the value of a library to the government of Pennsylvania. The passage of time has proven the legislators' wisdom in building an eclectic collection as well as a basic law library. Consequently, the finest Colonial Assembly library has grown with the care and nurture of succeeding generations of librarians to become the distinguished State Library of Pennsylvania.

NOTES

1 Library Company of Philadelphia, *The Charter, Laws, and Catalogue of Books of the Library Company of Philadelphia* (Philadelphia: Franklin & Hall, 1764).

2 Pennsylvania Assembly, *Votes and Proceedings of the House of Representatives of the Province of Pennsylvania* 6 vols. (Philadelphia, 1752-1776), 4:31.

3 Benjamin Franklin, *The Papers of Benjamin Franklin*, ed. Leonard W. Labaree [and others], 23 vols. (New Haven: Yale University Press, 1959-), 3:77.

4 Ibid.

5 *Votes and Proceedings*, 4:63.

6 Franklin, *Papers*, 3:213-214.

7 *Votes and Proceedings*, 4:90.

8 Franklin, *Papers*, 3:321.

9 "...N.B. Popples Map...It is the largest I ever saw, and the most distinct. Not very accurate. It is Eight foot square.—There is one in the Pensilvania State House." John Adams to Abigail Adams. Adams Family Archives, *Adams Family Correspondence* (Cambridge: Harvard University Press, Belknap Press, 1963), 2:91-92.

10 *Pennsylvania Magazine of History and Biography*, 42:217.

11 Library Company, *Charter*, p. 19.

12 Library Company of Philadelphia. Loganian Library, *First supplement to the Catalogue of Books belonging to the Loganian Library* (Philadelphia: Collins, 1867), p. x. Edwin Wolf, *At the Insistance of Benjamin Franklin* (Philadelphia: Library Company of Philadelphia, 1976), p. 19.

13 *Votes and Proceedings*, 4:213.

14 Ibid.

15 For the history of Isaac Norris II's library see Marie Elena Korey, *The Books of Isaac Norris (1701-1766) at Dickinson College* (Carlisle, PA: Dickinson College, 1976).

16 Isaac Norris to Robert Charles, 10 March 1753. Norris Letters, 1719-1756 (Norris Letters 9), pp. 32, 35. Historical Society of Pennsylvania.

17 Isaac Norris to Thomas Osborne and John Whiston, 16 March 1752. Isaac Norris Letterbook, 1735-1755 ("Wall Paper" Book), p. 70. Logan Collection #22, Historical Society of Pennsylvania.

18 Isaac Norris to Richard Partridge, 20 June 1752. Isaac Norris Letterbook, 1735-1755, p. 71.

19 *Votes and Proceedings*, 4:230.

20 Isaac Norris to Robert Charles, 10 March 1753. Norris Letters, 1719-1756, pp. 32, 35.

21 *Votes and Proceedings,* 4:237.

22 Isaac Norris to Robert Charles, 10 March 1753. Norris Letters, 1719-1756, pp. 32, 35.

23 Ibid.

24 Isaac Norris to Robert Charles, 27 March 1753. Norris Letters, 1719-1756, p. 38.

25 Ibid.

26 Isaac Norris to Robert Charles, 14 April 1753. Norris Letters, 1719-1756, p. 39.

27 Isaac Norris, "Norris Papers Account Book, 1747," p. 74. Library Company of Philadelphia Collection, Historical Society of Pennsylvania.

28 At this time the English pound sterling sold at an advance of seventy percent over the value of the Pennsylvania pound. Thus £500 sterling equalled £850 Pennsylvania currency.

29 Isaac Norris, "Norris of Fairhill Manuscripts General Loan Office Account Books, 1750-1768," p. 6. Historical Society of Pennsylvania.

30 Charles Norris (1712-1766) was a Trustee of the Loan Office and the brother of Isaac Norris II.

31 Isaac Norris, "Norris/Griffith Accountbook, 1722-55," p. [43]. Library Company of Philadelphia Collection, Historical Society of Pennsylvania.

32 Isaac Norris, "Isaac Norris Manuscript Account Book, Philadelphia, 1735-1765 (Flour Book, 1735)," p. 3. Library Company of Philadelphia Collection, Historical Society of Pennsylvania.

33 Isaac Norris, "Norris Papers Account Book, 1747," p. 77.

34 *Votes and Proceedings*, 4:267.

35 Isaac Norris, "Norris/Griffith Accountbook, 1722-55," p. 45.

36 Isaac Norris to William Logan. 14 November 1753. Isaac Norris Letterbook, 1735-1755 ("Wallpaper Book"), p. 74.

37 Isaac Norris. "Isaac Norris Ledger, 1736-66," p. 4. Library Company of Philadelphia Collection, Historical Society of Pennsylvania.

38 Isaac Norris to Robert Charles, 8 November 1753. "Norris Letter Book, 1719-1756," pp. 41-42.

39 Benjamin Franklin, "Record of Service in the Assembly," *Papers*, 4:155.

40 Isaac Norris, "Norris of Fairhill Manuscripts. General Loan Office Account Books, 1750-1768," p. 107.

41 *Votes and Proceedings*, 4:357.

42 Ibid.

43 Ibid, 4:445.

44 Andrew Burnaby, *Travels Through the Middle Settlements in North America, in the Years 1759 and 1760....* 2d ed. (London: T. Payne, 1775), p. 76.

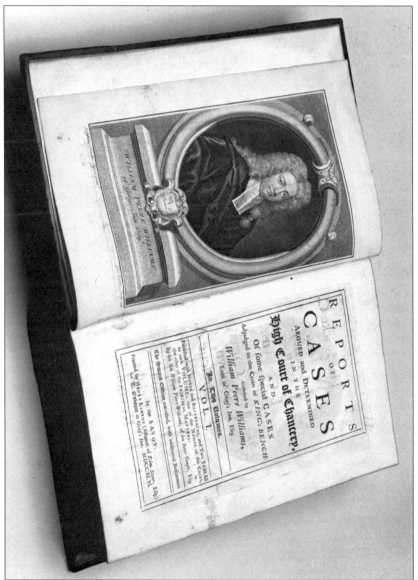

45 *Pennsylvania Gazette*, no. 592, 17 April 1740.

46 *Pennsylvania Gazette*, no. 1935, 23 January 1766.

47 *Pennsylvania Gazette*, no. 1960, 17 July 1766.

48 *Votes and Proceedings*, 5:509.

49 Ibid., 5:560.

50 Benjamin Franklin to a Committee of the Library Company. *Papers*, 19:270.

51 *Votes and Proceedings*, 6:422.

52 Ibid., 6:266.

53 Ibid., 6:424.

54 Ibid., 6:425.

55 Ibid.

56 *The Universal Magazine and Literary Museum*, 3 Oct. 1774, pp. 37-38. Norris Manuscript Collection #42, Historical Society of Pennsylvania.

57 John Adams, *Diary and Autobiography of John Adams* (Cambridge: Harvard University Press, Belknap Press, 1961), 3:323.

58 "Minutes of the Proceedings of the Convention of the State of Pennsylvania...." *Journals of the House of Representatives* (Philadelphia: Dunlap, 1782), p. 51.

59 [*Colonial Records of Pennsylvania*] (Harrisburg: T. Fenn, 1851-53), 11:309-310.

60 Pennsylvania General Assembly. *Journals of the House of Representatives* (Philadelphia: Dunlap, 1782), 1:157.

61 John Adams, *Familiar Letters of John Adams and His Wife Abigail Adams During the Revolution.* (New York: Hurd & Houghton, 1876), p. 314.

62 Timothy Matlack to Robert Levers, Easton, 1 October 1777. Catalog No. 2819, Independence National Historic Park Collection, Independence National Historic Park.

63 *Journals of the House of Representatives*, 1:288.

64 *Pennsylvania Archives*, First Series (Philadelphia: Severns, 1853), 5:754-755.

65 Ibid., 5:757.

66 Adams Family Archives, *Adams Family Correspondence*, 2:366n.

67 *Journals of the House of Representatives*, 1:287.

68 *Pennsylvania Archives*, 5:722.

69 *Journal of the House of Representatives*, 1:159.

70 Ibid., 1:243.

71 Ibid., 1:479.

72 Ibid., 1:480.

73 *Colonial Records*, 11:755.

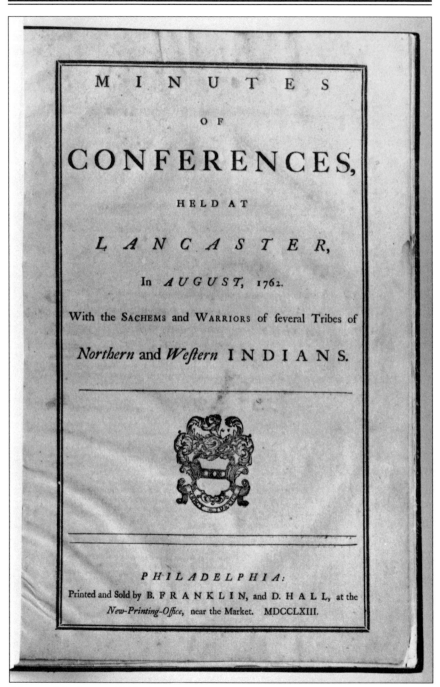

Minutes of Conferences, Held at Lancaster, In August, 1762. (Philadelphia: Franklin and Hall).

[74] Mr. Drayton was probably William Henry Drayton, a member of the Continental Congress from South Carolina. He began serving in Congress in March 1778 in York. His last day of attendance was 7 August 1779. He died 3 September 1779. William M. Dabney, *William Henry Drayton & the American Revolution* (Albuquerque: University of New Mexico Press, 1962), pp. 144-147.

[75] *Colonial Records*, 11:755.

[76] *The Pennsylvania Gazette and Weekly Advertiser*, no. 2550, 28 April 1779.

[77] Francois Jean, Marquis de Chastellux, *Travels in North America, in the Years 1780-81-82* (New York: White, Gallaher, & White, 1827), p. 109.

[78] Reference to Thomas Nevill, a house carpenter. Pennsylvania. Treasury Department, *A Brief View of the Accounts of the Treasury of Pennsylvania* (Philadelphia: Hall & Sellers, 1784), p. 95.

[79] *Colonial Records*, 12:588.

[80] Ibid., 12:699.

[81] Ibid., 13:576.

[82] Pennsylvania, General Assembly, *Minutes of the First Session of the Ninth General Assembly of the Commonwealth of Pennsylvania* (Philadelphia: Bailey, 1784), p. 37.

[83] Secretary Supreme Executive Council, 1786. Departmental Accounts, Box 13, RG4, Rec. Office of Comptroller General. Division of Archives and Manuscripts, Pennsylvania Historical and Museum Commission, Harrisburg, PA.

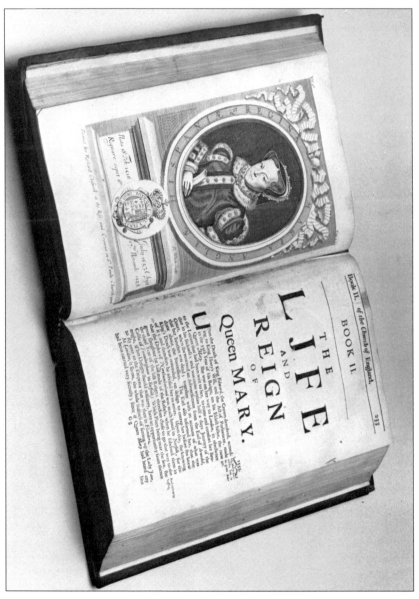

APPENDIX

On February 5, 1745/6 the Assembly of Pennsylvania ordered their clerk, Benjamin Franklin, "to send to England for the best Edition of the Statues at Large, for the Use of the House, and also for some large Maps (one of North America) to be hung up in the Assembly Room." This request created the foundation for one of the oldest and finest libraries not only in Pennsylvania, but in the nation. This expansive collection totalling 420 volumes covers a wide array of topics including books on English law, religion, mathematics, architecture, and history. This abbreviated list of titles from the General Assembly, Rare Books Collection eludes to the scope and diversity of topics that interested the lawmakers during the founding of the Commonwealth.

TITLE: An act for continuing and establishing the subsidie of tunnage and poundage, and for reviving an act for the better packing of butter, and redress of abuses therein. At the Parliament begun at Westminster the 17th day of September, Anno Domini 1656.

AUTHOR: England and Wales

PUBLISHED London: Printed by Henry Hills and John Field, Printers to His Highness, 1657.

TITLE: An act for limiting and setling the prices for wines: At Parliament begun at Westminster the 17th day of September, Anno Domini 1656.

AUTHOR: England and Wales

PUBLISHED: London: Printed by Henry Hills and John Field, Printers to His Highness, the Lord Protector, 1657.

TITLE: An act for quiet enjoying of sequestred parsonages and vicaridges by the present incumbent: at the Parliament begun at Westminster the 17th day of September, Anno Domini 1656.

AUTHOR: England and Wales.

PUBLISHED: London: Printed by Henry Hills and John Field, Printers to His Highness, the Lord Protector, 1657.

TITLE:	An act for the better observation of the Lords-Day. At the Parliament begun at Westminster the 17th day of September, Anno Domini 1656.
AUTHOR:	England and Wales.
PUBLISHED:	London: Printed by Henry Hills and John Field, Printers to His Highness, the Lord Protector, 1657.

TITLE:	An act for the preventing of the multiplicity of build ings in and about the suburbs of London, and within ten miles thereof: at the Parliament begun at Wesminster the 17th day of September, Anno Domini 1656.
AUTHOR:	England and Wales.
PUBLISHED:	London: Printed by Henry Hills and John Field, Printers to His Highness, the Lord Protector, 1657.

TITLE:	An act giving licence for transporting fish in forreign bottoms: at the Parliament begun at Westminster the 17th day of September, Anno Domini 1656.
AUTHOR:	England and Wales.
PUBLISHED	London: Printed by Henry Hills and John Field, Printers to His Highness, the Lord Protector, 1657.

TITLE:	The architecture of A. Palladio; in four books.
AUTHOR:	Palladio, Andrea, 1508-1580.
EDITION:	The 3d ed. cor. With notes and remarks of Inigo Jones.... And also, an appendix, containing The antiquities of Rome. Written by A. Palladio. And a discourse of the fires of the ancients...
PUBLISHED:	London: A. Ward <etc.> 1742.

TITLE:	A collection of debates, reports, orders and resolutions, of the House of Commons, touching the right of electing members to serve in Parliament, for the several counties, cities, burroughs, and towns corporate, in England and Wales: together with several ancient charters, and extracts, out of Domesday-Book, and other records, relating to the said right.

AUTHOR:	Bohun, William.
PUBLISHED:	London, Printed for Bernard Lintott and sold by Joshua Lintott <1702>.

TITLE:	A collection of the state papers of John Thurloe... Containing authentic memorials of the English affairs from the year 1638, to the restoration of King Charles II. Published from the originals, formerly in the library of John Lord Somers... and since in that of Sir Joseph Jekyll and papers, communicated by ... the Archbishop of Canterbury from the library at Lambeth... the Earl of Shelburn, and other hands. The whole digested into an exact order of time. To which is prefixed, The life of Mr. Thurloe: with a complete index to each volume.
AUTHOR:	Thurloe, John, 1616-1668.
PUBLISHED:	London, Printed for the executor of F. Gyles, 1742.

TITLE:	A complete system of geography. : Being a description of all the countries, islands, cities, chief towns, harbours, lakes, and rivers, mountains, mines, &c. of the known world. Shewing the situation, extent, and boundaries of the several empires, kingdoms, republics, principalities, provinces, &c. their climate, soil and produce ... and the distance and bearing of all the principal towns from one another. Including the most material revolutions and changes that have happen'd in every state.
AUTHOR:	Bowen, Emanuel, d. 1767.
PUBLISHED:	London: William Innys, etc., 1747.

TITLE:	A declaration of His Highness the Lord Protector and the Parliament, for a day of publique thanksgiving on Friday the twentieth of February 1656....
AUTHOR:	England and Wales. Lord Protector (1653-1658 : O. Cromwell).
PUBLISHED:	London: Printed by Henry Hills and John Field, Printers to His Highness the Lord Protector, 1656 <1657>.

TITLE:	Eight centuries of reports: or, eight hundred cases solemnly adjudged in the Exchequer-Chamber, or, upon writs of error.
AUTHOR:	Great Britain. Court of exchequer chamber.
EDITION:	The second edition corrected; to which is added a new table of the principal matters.
PUBLISHED:	\<London\> In the Savoy: Printed by E. and R. Nutt, and R. Gosling, (assigns of E. Sayer, Esq;) for John Worrall at the Dove in Bell-Yard near Lincoln's Inn; and Thomas Worrall at Judge Coke's Head against St. Dunstan's Church, Fleetstreet, 1734.

TITLE:	Le grand dictionaire historique: ou, Le malange curieux de l'histoire sacree et profane
AUTHOR:	Moreri, Louis, 1643-1680.
EDITION:	18 e et derniere ed., re., cor. & augm. tres consider ablement.
PUBLISHED:	Amsterdam: Chez P. Brunel \<etc.\>, 1740.

TITLE:	Haklvytvs posthumus or Pvrchas his Pilgrimes. Contayning a history of the world, in sea voyages, and lande-trauells.
AUTHOR:	Purchas, Samuel, 1577?-1626.
PUBLISHED:	London, Imprinted for H. Fetherston, 1625.

TITLE:	Historical collections: or, An exact account of the proceedings of the four last parliaments of Q. Elizabeth of famous memory. Wherein is contained the compleat journals both of the Lords and Commons, taken from the original records of their houses. As also the more particular behaviours of the worthy members during all the last notable sessions together with the most considerable passages of the history of those times.
AUTHOR:	Townshend, Hayward, b. 1577.
PUBLISHED:	London, Printed for T. Basset, W. Crooke, and W. Cademan, 1680.

TITLE: The journals of all the Parliaments during the reign of Queen Elizabeth, both of the House of Lords and House of Commons.

AUTHOR: D'Ewes, Simonds, Sir, 1602-1650.

EDITION: Rev. and publ. by Paul Bowes.

PUBLISHED: London, Printed for John Starkey at the Mitre in Fleetstreet near Temple-Bar. 1682.

TITLE: Laws of the government of New-Castle, Kent and Sussex upon Delaware.

AUTHOR: Delaware (Colony) Laws, statutes, etc.

PUBLISHED: Philadelphia, Printed by B. Franklin, 1741.

TITLE: Laws of the government of New-Castle, Kent and Sussex upon Delaware.

AUTHOR: Delaware (Colony) Laws, statutes, etc.

PUBLISHED: Philadelphia, Printed by B. Franklin and D. Hall, 1752.

TITLE: The laws, ordinances, and institutions of the Admiralty of Great Britain, civil and military: comprehending, I. Such ancient naval laws and customs as are still in use. II. An abstract of the statutes in force relating to maritime affairs and commerce. III. The marine treaties at large. IV. A critical account of naval affairs and commerce, from the regin of Alfred the Great. V. The present state of the navey, and of the officers, offices, ships, etc. thereof, interspersed with dissertations, notes and comments, for the use of the officers of the navy, masters of ships, mariners, merchants, insurers, and the trading part of the nation in general, with a preface, giving a more particular account of the nature, use and design of this work. In two volumes.

AUTHOR: Great Britain. Admiralty.

PUBLISHED: London: Printed for A. Millar, 1746.

TITLE:	Le beau-pledeur: A book of entries, containing declarations, information, and other select and approved pleadings: with special verdicts and demurrers, in most actions, real, personal, and mixt, which have been argued and adjudged in the most courts at Westminster: Together with faithful references to the most authentick printed law-books now extant, where the cases of these entries are reported: and a more copious and useful table than hath been hitherto printed in any book of entries: The whole comprehending the very art and method of good pleading.
AUTHOR:	Winch, Humphrey, Sir, 1555?-1625.
PUBLISHED:	London: Printed by George Sawbridge, William Rawlins, and Samuel Roycroft.. for Thomas Basset.. Richard Chiswell, and Benjamin Tooke..,1680.

TITLE:	Mathematical elements of natural philosophy confirm'd by experiments: or, An introduction to Sir Isaac Newton's philosophy
AUTHOR:	Gravesande, Willem Jacob van's, 1688-1742.
EDITION:	The sixth edition greatly improved by the Author, and illustrated with 127 Copper Plates all new engraven.
PUBLISHED:	London: Printed for W. Innys, T. Longman and T. Shewell, C,. Hitch, in Pater-Noster-Row; and M. Senex, in Fleet-Street, M.DCC.XLVII.

TITLE:	Memorials of the English affairs; or, An historical account of what passed from the beginning of the reign of Charles the First, to King Charles the Second his happy restauration. Containing the publick transactions, civil and military. Together with the private consultations and secrets of the cabinet.
AUTHOR:	Whitelocke, Bulstrode, Sir, 1605-1675.
EDITION:	New ed., with many additions never before printed.
PUBLISHED:	London, Printed for J. Tonson, 1732.

TITLE:	Modern cases, argued and adjudged in the Court of Queen's bench at Westminster, in the second and third

years of Queen Anne <1703-1704> in the time when Sir John Holt sate chief justice there. With two tables: the first, of the names of the cases: and the other, of the special matter therein contained.

AUTHOR: Great Britain. Court of King's Bench.

EDITION: The 2d ed. Review'd and corrected, and many thousand new and proper references added. By W. B., esq.

PUBLISHED: <London> In the Savoy, Printed by E. Nutt, and R. Gosling for D. Browne <etc.> 1719.

TITLE: The naval history of England, in all its branches; from the Norman Conquest in the year 1066, to the conclusion of 1734.

AUTHOR: Lediard, Thomas, 1685-1743.

PUBLISHED: London, Printed for J. Wilcox <etc.> 1735.

TITLE: A new law-dictionary: containing the interpretation and definition of words and terms used in the law, as also the whole law and practice thereof, under all the proper heads and titles, together with such information relating thereto as explain the history and antiquity of the law, and our manners, customs, and original government, collected and abstracted from all dictionaries, abridgments, institutes, reports, year-books, charters, registers, chronicles, and histories....

AUTHOR: Jacob, Giles, 1686-1744.

EDITION: 8th ed. The law proceedings being done into English, with great additions and improvements from the latest reports and statutes to this time, to which is annexed a table of references to all the arguments and resolution of the Lord Chief Justice Holt in the several volumes of reports.

PUBLISHED: <London> In the Savoy: Printed by H. Woodfall and W. Strahan for T. Osborne <etc.>, 1762.

TITLE: A New pandect of Roman civil law, as anciently established in that new empire; and now received and practised in most European nations: with many useful observations theron; shewing, wherein that law differs from the municipal laws of Great Britain, from the canon law in general, and from that part of it now in use here with us in England.

AUTHOR: Ayliffe, John, 1676-1732.

PUBLISHED: London, Printed for T. Osborne in Grays Inn, 1734.

TITLE: Of the law of nature and nations: Eight books

AUTHOR: Pufendorf, Samuel, freiherr von, 1632-1694.

EDITION: The 4th ed., carefully corrected. To which is now prefixed Mr. Barbeyrac's prefatory discourse, containing An historical and critical account of the science of mortality... Done into English by Mr. Carew...

PUBLISHED: London: J. Walthoe, R. Wilkin <etc.>, 1729.

TITLE: An order of His Highness, with the advice and consent of his Privy Council, for continuing the committee for the army: and for the more orderly paiment and issuing forth of the three moneths assessment of sixty thousand pounds by the moneth, commencing the 25th of March, 1657: at the Council at Whitehall, the 14th of July 1657.

AUTHOR: England and Wales. Lord Protector (1653-1658 : O. Cromwell)

PUBLISHED: London: Printed by Henry Hills and John Field, Printers to His Highness the Lord Protector, 1657.

TITLE: The rights of war and peace, in three books. Wherein are explained, the law of nature and nations, and the principle points relating to government.

AUTHOR: Grotius, Hugo, 1583-1645.

PUBLISHED: London, Printed for W. Innys <etc.> 1738.

TITLE: Rules for drawing the several parts of architecture, in a more exact and easy manner than has been hereto fore practiced, by which all fractions, in dividing the principal members and their parts, are avoided.

AUTHOR: Gibbs, James, 1682-1754.

EDITION: The 3d ed.

PUBLISHED: London, W. Innys <etc.> 1753.

TITLE: A True narrative of the late success which it hath pleased God to give to some part of the fleet of this common-wealth, upon the Spanish coast, against the king of Spains West-India fleet, in its return to Cadiz: being the substance, of several letters writ and sent by the generals of the fleet upon this occasion. Saturday, the 4. of October, 1656. Ordered by the Parliament, that this narrative be forthwith printed and published.

AUTHOR: England and Wales.

PUBLISHED: London, Printed by Henry Hills, and John Field, printers to His Highness, the Lord Protector, 1656.

TITLE: The works of Francis Bacon, Baron of Verulam, Viscount St. Alban, and Lord High Chancellor of England.

AUTHOR: Bacon, Francis, 1561-1626

PUBLISHED: London, Printed for A. Millar, 1753.

TITLE: The works of John Locke... To which is added, the life of the author and a collection of several of his pieces published by Mr. Desmaizeaux.

AUTHOR: Locke, John 1632-1704.

EDITION: 5th ed.

PUBLISHED: London, Printed for S. Birt <etc.> 1751.

TITLE: The works of Sir William Temple, Bart, In two volumes ... To which is prefixed, The life and character of Sir William Temple.

AUTHOR: Temple, William, Sir, 1628-1699.

PUBLISHED: London: Printed for T. Woodward, S. Birt, J. and P. Knapton, J. Clark, T. Wotton, J. Shuckburg, D. Brown, H. Lintot, J. and R. Tonson and S. Draper, C. Bathurst, M. Mears, and the Executor of J. Round. MDCCL.

TITLE:	The works of the honourable Robert Boyle. In five volumes. To which is prefixed the life of the author.
AUTHOR:	Boyle, Robert, 1627-1691.
PUBLISHED:	London, Printed for A. Millar, 1744.

A Parent's Guide to Living with Teens
Jacob P. Heerema

CALL ME WHEN YOU'RE 20!

CRC Publications
Grand Rapids, Michigan

Cover photograph: Peter De Ritter

Heerema, Jacob P., 1937-
    Call me when you're 20!: a parent's guide to living with teens / Jacob
P. Heerema.
        p. c.m.—(Issues in Christian living)
    Includes bibliographical references.
    ISBN 1-56212-009-3 $5.75
    1. Parent and teenager—United States. 2. Communication in the
family—United States. 3. Child rearing—Religious aspects—
Christianity. I. Title. II. Series.
HQ799.15.H44 1991
306.874—dc20   91-34248
    CIP

ISBN 1-56212-009-3
9 8 7 6 5 4 3 2 1

CONTENTS

Introduction 5

One: A Two-Way Street 7
Two: When Adolescents Act Like Teenagers 21
Three: Fights Over Fairness 33
Four: When Family Ties No Longer Bind 45
Five: The Quest to Be Blest 57
Six: Paint Them a Rainbow 69

Suggested Reading List 85

INTRODUCTION

Reading this book is not like undergoing major surgery. It's more like submitting to a thorough physical. I believe Christ places the highest regard on quality family life. So I'm inviting you to sit back and reflect on the way things are going at your home.

Most parents readily acknowledge that parenting teenagers is tough. We will be taking a look at some of the issues that trigger teens' tempers and bring parents pain.

I've drawn this material together while serving as chaplain to troubled teens at the Pine Rest Christian Hospital (Grand Rapids, MI). As part of my work here, I've had the privilege of listening to hundreds of teens who feel that either they have failed their families or their families have failed them. Many of them come from dysfunctional or single-parent homes, but a good number of them also come from intact families. A troubled teen is often the symptom-bearer of a family in need of help.

Teens usually do a good job of getting our attention. The particular issues may have to do with curfew, music, booze, schoolwork, who pays for car insurance (after their first accident!), or spring break. Behind these issues, though, is an underlying need in these adolescents to feel accepted and affirmed as emerging adults. Emancipation is not only predictable but appropriate, and parents must acknowledge their teens' right to grow up. But parents are also right in underscoring their teens' responsibility to grow up as servants of Christ. That's where the struggles come in. Our goal is to have them join us in honoring Jesus as Lord of our lives.

Perhaps you've heard this story before: A family is seated at their favorite restaurant. Mom and Dad look over the menu while eight-year-old Jimmy counts the silverware. The waitress takes Mom's and Dad's orders and then asks Jimmy what he would like. While he's telling her he would like a hot dog and fries, Mom interrupts to say, "He'll have a hamburger and a tossed salad." The waitress looks at Jimmy and asks, "And what would you like on your hot dog?" As she walks off to the kitchen, Jimmy taps his mother on the arm and says, "She's neat! She thinks I'm real!"

Our teens need to know that we think they're real too. So in this book we will take a look at our family communication systems. We'll also look at appropriate responses to unpredictable teen behaviors. We'll look at how peer pressure, sexuality, substance abuse, sports, and studies fit into the challenging world of adolescence. Through it all, our teens need to be sure that we know they're real . . . and that we love them!

Responsible parenting is never easy. It can be enjoyable, but it's never easy. Authentic parenting happens when older children of the Lord (parents) coach and encourage younger children (adolescents) to live life *in God's presence*. Parents of teens need to distinguish between being intimate but not intrusive, being ever-present but not overly protective, and focusing on counsel rather than control. When parents and teens honestly struggle together to discern the Lord's will, the key word will not be *survival* but *celebration*. It's my prayer that your family life will be something you don't just endure but really enjoy!

—Jacob P. Heerema

ONE

A TWO-WAY STREET

Are You Still There?

It's about 11:45 P.M., and your son is due in at midnight. It's a big night for him: you let him use the new car, his school's football team could clinch the trophy by winning the game, and he's taking Joy out for the first time. You would normally be sleeping by now, but tonight is special. You're eager to hear about Tim's big night.

You've always felt pretty good about the way Tim and his two younger brothers communicate with you. Up until a few months ago you were sure there was an open line of communication between you and the kids. But lately Tim has been sending out different signals. He seems to be holding back a bit—not initiating conversations with you the way he used to. In fact, at times he seems to be avoiding you when you'd really like to talk. You're hoping he'll feel free to talk tonight.

You hear the garage door open. The car pulls in, and the engine stops. Tim comes in through the kitchen door, hangs up the keys in the hallway, and calls out, "I made it by twelve! See you in the morning!" He starts heading up the stairs to his room. You call out, inviting him to come back down and talk for a few minutes about how things went. You have a long list of questions: Did the car work OK? What does he think of his new girlfriend? Who won the game? He grudgingly produces a few abbreviated answers to your questions. He tells you that the car did OK, and Joy is OK, and

7

that his team was not OK. They lost. He gives you the facts, but none of his feelings. "So can I go to bed now?" he asks.

You and your spouse share your disappointment about this new trend. It was so much nicer when Tim enjoyed sitting around and talking with you about the little details of his everyday life. Ever since he started high school, he seems to have been pulling back from family life. It's like getting a bad connection when you make a long-distance call. You start to talk, but then the static interrupts the conversation. You wait for a moment and ask, "Are you still there?"

What's New with Tim?

Tim is moving into his adolescent years, a period marked by change. He's experiencing a long-awaited and eagerly anticipated physical transformation. He's developing the ability to go beyond an earlier stage of concrete thinking when tough questions had simple answers, and he's considering new alternatives. He wonders more now, so he's questioning some of the things you'd like him to accept. His social world is expanding too. He has new friends, including an interesting new girlfriend. And he's definitely much more in touch with his peers than with his parents.

So what's new with Tim? His *whole world* is new, because it's expanding. Tim's world of adolescence is a world of discovery and exploration.

Parenting is something like the launching of a satellite. Children, like space capsules, are very dependent on their "rockets"—the power source that carries them. But the long-range objective of the launch is to thrust the capsule into orbit. Adolescents are coming closer to the time when they will be able to travel on their own, and parents ought to celebrate that achievement. Our goal as Christian parents is to provide a loving and nurturing environment for our children so that they will become mature adults.

Adolescents are busy shedding some of the rockets that have carried them to this stage of the journey. Their eagerness to experiment with emancipation is an endorsement of your effectiveness as a caring parent. You have given them a sense of purpose in life. You have contributed to their sense of self-esteem. Now you are giving them permission to grow up—a process that is painful for teens as well as for their parents.

Does Growing Up Have to Hurt?

It's a warm Saturday morning. Dad is up at 7 A.M., puts on a pot of coffee, and takes off for his four-mile run. He comes back home, pours his coffee, then knocks on Carol's door so that she will have time to get ready for their weekly breakfast together at the restaurant of her choice.

Carol's in ninth grade now, and they've been doing this since she was six years old. Dad showers and gets dressed, then discovers that Carol hasn't come downstairs yet. He goes back to her room and knocks again on her door. He's surprised to hear her say she doesn't really feel like going today.

"But honey, we've been doing this for almost ten years. What's up?" Carol lifts her head toward Dad and says, "I just don't feel like going through another interrogation! I'd rather sleep in. Maybe we can talk some other time."

Dad is caught off guard, and he's hurt. He's been operating on the assumption that he'll be able to maintain good communication with Carol by simply keeping in touch with her on a regular basis. But Carol is changing. She is no longer the little girl who thinks it's great to talk about everything with Daddy the way she used to. She has become very involved with her friends at school and in the church youth group. When they get together, they can talk for hours about all the things that matter to them—what they think about other kids, what they think about their teachers, and what they think about their parents. They've also decided that it's not "cool" to talk all these things over with parents anymore. So breakfast with Dad on Saturday mornings is out for now.

Dad has to learn that yesterday's coupons will not be honored at today's sale. Good communication, like a sky full of clouds, keeps changing. Carol knows and appreciates that Dad loves her and places a high priority on keeping in touch with her. But right now she is banking on that love by taking the risk of declining his invitation for breakfast. Carol is really saying that her parents have set her free to reach beyond her family circle for friends. It's not that she's saying "no" to family. Rather, she is secure enough about her place in the family to research her place in a wider world. She is really learning to say "yes" to a bigger family.

Why Not Fix Pizza at Home?

Judy is turning thirteen, and for her birthday she wants to do something special with her group of eight friends. Mom has offered to have them all over for a slumber party and to fix pizzas for the whole group. She has even offered to prepare the snacks, plan some games, and rent a few videos for the group to watch. But as the time gets closer, Judy tells her mom that the girls would rather meet at the mall, buy their pizza there, and just walk around for several hours "having fun and talking."

Judy's mom is upset. "Why don't you want your friends to come here?" she asks in a hurt voice. Judy again explains that the girls prefer to go to the mall.

9

Here we have another example of a caring parent who is caught off guard by the SOS (Signal of Struggle) message being sent by her daughter. Perhaps Judy is serving notice that she is troubled by *smother love*. If Judy accepts her mother's offer of having the party at home, it will be Mother's party rather than Judy's. As an emerging adolescent, Judy would like to have her ideas and opinions honored. She would like to play a major role in the planning of her own special event.

At this point it's important that Judy's mom try to figure out what's really going on before responding. It's important that she examine her own motives as well as her daughter's. Judy may be sending a fairly clear message about where she is on the journey toward emancipation. She may be calling for understanding, for space to make more of her own decisions and to explore her expanding world. By endorsing Judy's desire to enjoy the world beyond her home, Mother may be fostering the kind of maturity she wants to cultivate in Judy's life.

What Makes for Good Communication?

Take a minute to reflect on the times when you felt you really enjoyed good communication with another person. More than likely, they were times when you believed your feelings were sincerely honored by the person with whom you were talking. In good communication it is not imperative for both parties to agree, but it is essential that they respect and honor each other's opinions and feelings at all times.

Christian families are called to create an atmosphere in which this kind of mutual acceptance and respect undergirds all interactions. Whenever any members of the family, young or old, take the risk of revealing their feelings or ideas, they should be treated with love and respect by other family members. Young children, for example, should not be criticized for their tears (e.g., "Don't be such a baby!"). Instead, parents should acknowledge a child's sadness and pursue the reason for the tears, thus affirming the child's right to feel sorrow. This approach assures children that when they reveal their feelings, whether happy or sad, others are willing to understand and accept them.

When their opinions are ignored, belittled, or judged as stupid, children will gradually learn to withhold their ideas. The same is true for feelings. If revealing emotions predictably generates put-downs and judgments from parents, children will learn to keep feelings of sadness, guilt, and fear secret. They will grow up assuming that communication is a one-way street on which parents send the messages while children only listen.

Communication must always be a *two-way* street. Christian parents are called to encourage children to express all the gifts that make them imagebearers of God. Their opinions, their fears, their questions, their feelings, and their hopes should always be honored in the dialogue that fills the sound track of family life.

All of us must realize that the nature of our relationship with our teenagers in many ways reflects the quality of our communication with them during their earlier years. If love and mutual respect have been quite consistently expressed, teenagers will feel secure enough to reach beyond the dependable love of family to the less predictable love of their expanding world. They will know that even if they sometimes spurn family ties, their parents will continue to keep their promise to love them into adulthood.

Our teens are banking on that love—even if they can't always say so! The kind of love that fosters open communication includes at least the following features:

1. Willingness to see one another as persons . . . always

It is essential to remember that parents and teenagers are children of God, bearers of God's image who are called to new life in Christ. Neither parents nor children should ever think of each other as mere objects. We are all God's special children.

2. Willingness to surrender all control to the Lord

It is important to acknowledge, as parents, that we live under the lordship of Jesus. It is his will we seek to express in our lives, and it is his will we encourage our children to express. Perhaps our quest for control will be modified and our tendency to criticize and condemn our children will be offset by the humble awareness that we are all erring children of a forgiving Lord. This insight will deliver us from the myth of always having to be "perfect" parents. We are free to acknowledge our mistakes to one another within our families.

3. Willingness to trust one another

It is important for parents to trust their children, even if their behavior at times calls that trust into question. If a child has stolen something, told a lie, or withheld information, truth has been tarnished. The parent should help the child see the implications of dishonesty for future relationships. Open communication is threatened when trust has been violated.

However, parents should not dwell on memories of bad moments. If a child admits to telling a lie and apologizes, the slate should be erased. The parent should once again accept the child

11

as a truth-teller, so that future communication is not hampered by the memory of yesterday's failure to tell the truth.

I have met a number of teenagers who readily admit they have told lies to their parents because of shame or fear of punishment. When their parents discovered the dishonesty, the teens were punished. But they were also slandered. "I'll never be able to trust you again!" their parents told them. These teens insist that it makes no difference anymore whether they tell the truth or not—their parents will not believe them anyway. A teenager loses interest in being trustworthy if a parent is unwilling to trust him or her.

Trying Hard to Keep in Touch

One of the ways that Christian families traditionally keep in touch with one another is by sharing mealtimes together. We all know how difficult this is in a society in which work schedules, school commitments, recreational activities, sports events, and church programs send us off in many different directions. However, I don't think we should ever underestimate the importance of maintaining family mealtimes. We should make a concerted effort to have as many meals together as possible, encouraging all family members to be present for these important occasions.

This regular experience keeps lines of communication open between parents and children, brothers and sisters. Mealtime conversations are often devoted to a wide range of seemingly insignificant topics, but the very routine of processing these things as a family keeps us in touch with one another. Parents should make a special effort to direct these conversations in such a way that every family member has the opportunity to report the high points and the low points of his or her day. Joys should be celebrated and sadness shared. Mealtime conversations become a model for the kind of open communication of thoughts and feelings we should strive to achieve within our families.

Earlier in this chapter we raised the question of whether planned or unscheduled communication is best. I believe parents should be open to both approaches. Think of ways to plan special times for personal conversation with each of your children—times when they can count on having the full and undivided attention of a parent who is personally interested in them. But also be alert to special opportunities for meaningful conversation that may come up from time to time. Your daughter may come home from a date, for example, and hint that she needs to talk. Although you are very tired, you may sense that this is a golden opportunity to hear her out on the things that are most important to her at this time. Out of such a conversation may emerge unmatched opportunities to talk about her self-esteem, fear of being rejected by her closest friends, questions about her sexuality, career plans, or worries about her school performance. Parents need to pray for wisdom to identify such special moments for good communication.

In his book *You Can Be a Great Parent*, Charlie Shedd lists six promises he made to his son Peter on the day he was born—and read and reread to Peter at various stages of his growing up. One of the promises he made was this: "I promise to really be with you when I am with you!"

Our teenagers need to hear that same promise from us, and they need to hear us repeat it often. That doesn't mean that whenever we're with our children, we should be pressuring them into heavy conversations. It means that when we're together, we do all we can to make the interaction a genuine expression of our interest and love. It means that if they want to talk, we will make ourselves available. And it means that if they are talking, we will *really* listen—not only with our ears but also with our hearts.

Can Parents Try Too Hard to Keep in Touch?

Yes, they can. We all do at times, I'm sure.

Usually parents' efforts to communicate are motivated by love for their children. However, our motives can often become mixed. Sometimes what we think of as love is mixed with pride or fear. For example, we cherish the privilege of being able to report our son's scholastic, social, and sports achievements to such an extent that we press him (or his friends) for details he may not wish to disclose. Or our hidden fear of a daughter's sexual improprieties may lead us to call the school counselor to see if she has discussed birth control with him. Yes, sometimes parents can try too hard.

Karen and her mother have been having trouble for more than a year now. How different from when Karen was younger! Mother and Karen used to be able to talk about almost anything. Now there are some subjects they hardly dare bring up—subjects such as Karen's grade in Advanced Algebra, her poor driving record, and her heavy dating with Mark. And lately Karen has been insisting that her mother stay out of her room. She calls it her private space.

One day Karen forgets to throw her sheets in the wash, so her mother goes in to take them from the bed. And that's when she sees Karen's journal . . . sitting right out there on her desk, with her pen stuck between the pages where she wrote her last entry. Karen's mother can't help but take a quick peek. She scans that page, and then turns back a few pages. She is shocked . . . horrified . . . distraught! If these entries come anywhere near to being true, her worst suspicions are confirmed. She now knows of her

13

daughter's sexual intimacies with Mark, her fear of being pregnant, and her consideration of an abortion.

Karen's mother now faces a dilemma. The lines of communication with Karen are so strained that any disagreement between them leads to a major clash. As it is, Karen always accuses her mom of prying . . . so what should she do? Perhaps she should confront Karen as soon as she comes home from school. Or maybe she should call the school counselor to share this information with him. Maybe she should let their pastor know. Maybe she should call her husband—even though she's afraid the news might lead him to say and do things he will regret for the rest of his life. What would be the best way to handle the problem?

Karen's story accurately reflects the situation in hundreds of homes in our communities. In such homes it's obvious that lines of communication have been strained already for many years and that no single action will bring a quick remedy to such dysfunctional families. Certainly Karen and her parents need ample opportunity to sit down together to come to mutual understandings. They have a great need for a healing of the hurts that have driven them apart.

But Karen's mother has to be careful about violating trust with her daughter. She has invaded Karen's private space. She has intruded on her daughter's private world. My sense is that she should not use the information she garnered from snooping in Karen's journal as the basis for a confrontation. Rather, she should initiate a process by which, through the assistance of a neutral third party (such as the family pastor, a school counselor, or a therapist), the family might be able to discover a way to keep in touch as Karen moves with determination toward emancipation.

God wants members of families to be candid and open with one another, always. But the Bible admonishes us to always speak the truth in love. I believe that as parents we must pray for the Spirit's wisdom to develop a keen sense of timing. There are times to speak and times to be silent. In faithfully weaning children, parents should never lose sight of the fact that we are called to encourage children to grow up into adulthood. That means we should be willing to let go of them in the assurance that their heavenly Father will never let go of them.

So it's not enough to say that parenting brings children from dependence to independence. Adolescence is an experiment in independence which, with God's help, will bring teens to a new awareness of their dependence on God and to a celebration of their interdependence with all the children in the family of Christ's love.

14

Suggestions for Group Session

Getting Started

It might be helpful for members of the group to introduce themselves, telling a little bit about family life in their childhood, perhaps describing the communication they remember taking place between themselves and their parents when they were teenagers. Members could then go on to describe their present family situation. It would be helpful for the group to know how many participants are currently parenting teenagers.

Scripture Readings
> Proverbs 4:24
> 1 Corinthians 13:4-6
> Ephesians 4:15
> Ephesians 4:25-32
> James 1:19

Opening Prayer

After you have read the Scripture verses together, allow time for each group member to write down two or three basic principles of communication they find in these passages. After a few minutes share your ideas, and keep these important principles in mind as you proceed with this lesson on communication between parents and teens. Pray together that God may open the channels of communication not only between parents and teens but also between members of this group.

For Discussion

What Makes a Family Healthy?

Take time to identify more specifically some of the things group members appreciated about their childhood family life. Then take an informal poll to identify the features of strong families that your group considers to be most important.

Dolores Curran wrote a fine book entitled *Traits of a Healthy Family*, in which she reports the results of responses she received from more than five hundred persons who work with families—including educators, pastors, health-care providers, family counselors, and leaders of community volunteer agencies. The respondents all worked directly with families they considered healthy. Here are the fifteen traits they selected, in the order in which they were most often chosen.

The healthy family . . .

- communicates and listens.
- affirms and supports one another.
- teaches respect for others.
- develops a sense of trust.
- has a sense of play and humor.
- exhibits a sense of shared responsibility.
- teaches a sense of right and wrong.
- has a strong sense of family in which rituals and traditions abound.
- has a balance of interaction among members.
- has a shared religious core.
- respects the privacy of one another.
- values service to others.
- fosters family table time and conversation.
- shares leisure time.
- admits to and seeks help with problems.

1. Compare Curran's list with the one your group developed.

2. Which items on her list do you think are wrongly placed—in other words, which items do you believe should be closer to the top or the bottom because they are of greater or lesser significance than the survey reveals? Explain and defend your changes.

3. Why do you think good communication was chosen as the most important trait of a healthy family?

What Is It Like at Home?

We shift now from general thoughts about communication to some real-life experiences of parents in the group as they seek to maintain good communication with their teenage children. Group members should respond to the following three questions:

4. Has communication between you and your children become more difficult as they have moved into adolescence? Explain.

5. What are some of the things that seem to work well for you in keeping lines of communication open?

6. Describe a situation in which it seemed you and your teen were miles apart. Could you rebuild the lines of communication? If so, how?

7. You've had the opportunity to learn a bit more about one another's family life, and you have undoubtedly learned some good things from sharing what is already taking place in your homes. As you think of ways to maintain good communication with your teens, you may wish to consider and discuss some of these suggestions offered by authors dealing with family life. Evaluate the value of each of the following approaches:

a. *Guided conversation at designated mealtimes.* Leadership may rotate among all family members. The focus is on reporting and sharing information about each person's dreams and disappointments. Approaches to these guided discussions might include some of the following:

 • The neatest thing that happened to me today was . . .

 • I felt most loved today when . . .

 • Something I wish hadn't happened this week was . . .

 • The thing I like best about each of you is . . .

b. *The weekly family council.* Many counselors and authors recommend this idea. All family members are urged to participate in the council. Discussion goes beyond mere reporting to a review of family issues introduced by both children and parents. Problem areas and differences of opinion on issues such as curfew are openly discussed.

c. *The weekly interview.* A parent meets separately with each child on a weekly basis, thus guaranteeing each child a place in his or her parents' busy schedules. (Susannah Wesley, mother of eighteen children—including the famous preachers and hymnwriters, John and Charles Wesley—held weekly conferences with each one of her children!)

d. *Have ears, will listen.* This approach involves no planned conversations but stresses an often-repeated promise and reminder that any family member will talk with any other family member when requested to do so.

e. *The family journal.* A notebook is available for everyone's use. All family members are encouraged to document questions, comments, opinions, and reactions to recent family experiences. The journal is reviewed regularly by all, which encourages follow-up conversations.

f. *Note-writing.*This approach may work well for those who feel less comfortable talking about their feelings. A simple note, placed in a teen's room (or even sent by mail) may effectively

17

communicate your love and concern in a time of special need.

What Do You Think?

8. The chapter you read in preparation for this session presented several problem situations that may reflect some of the tough situations you've faced in your own families. Your group may wish to select one or two of these for further discussion.

9. Is it possible to fall into the trap of over-parenting our teens? Our need to know their thoughts, feelings, and plans may at times lead us to disregard appropriate boundaries. What do you think?

10. Wise parents encourage openness and disclosure, but they also respect each child's right, and need, for privacy. Keeping that in mind, evaluate each of the following parental actions. When, if ever, might each be appropriate? Inappropriate?

- listening in on a teen's phone conversation
- eavesdropping on a teen's conversation with friends in another room
- insisting that your teen let you know where he or she is going on a weekend evening
- asking your teen to keep his or her room clean
- questioning a teen's friends or younger brothers and sisters to find out more about a suspicious situation
- inspecting their private turf (a closet or the trunk of a car) for evidence of misbehaviors
- objecting to the friends your teen hangs around with

11. What about those times when a sharing session ends up as a shouting match? Most of us tend to avoid conflict, but disagreements are inevitable, especially when we are dealing with young people who are moving into adulthood. To avoid conflict at all costs will greatly diminish the likelihood of open communication in any relationship. Evaluate this quote:

We need to recognize the importance of maintaining a relationship no matter how much these youngsters might upset us. The contact need not always be positive. The opposite of love, after all, is not hate, but indifference. A relationship—even an adversarial one—is better than no relationship at all. Remaining in communication rather than brooding silently, staying engaged with these youths rather than pulling away, and being committed to enhancing their

18

welfare—in spite of their recalcitrance and recidivism—rather than becoming bitter and giving up makes an enormous difference in the lives of these young people.

—Teenagers—When to Worry and What to Do, Douglas H. Powell; New York: Doubleday, 1987; p. 51.

Closing

You may wish to close today with sentence prayers, each of you asking for God's help, either in general or specific terms, in communicating with your children—in knowing when to speak out and when to keep silent.

TWO

WHEN ADOLESCENTS ACT LIKE TEENAGERS

One of the exciting gifts many teens offer their middle-aged parents is the element of surprise. Sometimes the surprises are pleasant and encouraging to parents. Far more often they're the kind of bombshells that you knew dropped on other people's families but never expected to fall on your own. All of a sudden family life seems to be seriously strained.

Do any of these sound familiar?

- Sara signs up for a correspondence course with a New Age group.
- Kevin comes home wearing a pierced earring.
- Jane announces that she and her friends have reserved a motel room in Florida during spring break.
- Steve quietly mentions at dinner that he has dropped out of the school choir.

These impulsive thoughts and actions are common enough among adolescents that they deserve our further consideration. Let's take a closer look at some real-life examples of these sudden shifts in belief and behavior that teenagers frequently lay at the feet of their sometimes stunned parents.

So What's the Big Deal?

Alan swims well, and he has lots of friends. You find his wet bathing suit draped over the kitchen counter on Saturday morning and discover later (when he emerges from his room) that late Friday evening he and his three buddies went for a dip at the gravel pit. You can't believe he did it! It's unsafe, and he knows it. It's clearly posted as private property, and he knows that too. You confront him with his foolish behavior: breaking curfew, breaking the law, and risking his life. The only response you get is "So what's the big deal?"

Jenna is doing extremely well at school and has a shot at becoming valedictorian if she maintains her GPA for her final year of high school. You're amazed that she can play on the basketball team and still carry her school load so well. She's even been taking honors English for extra credit. That's why you're so shocked when she comes home and announces that she's dropped that course. She claims to have lost interest in it. And besides, she wants to spend more of her free time with Tom. They've been going together for half a year now and are getting increasingly serious about their relationship. You challenge her on this decision and demand that she reconsider. Her only response is "So what's the big deal?"

Michael has never given you any major problems. He's maintaining a B average at school, has a small circle of good friends, and enjoys the youth group at church. He comes home one Sunday night and informs you that he has just signed up for a summer SWIM assignment, which means he will have to quit his fifty-hour-per-week summer job with the landscaping crew. You're taken totally by surprise. Just yesterday he told you he was planning to use his summer earnings to pay off his car and carry half the costs of his first year in college. How can he change his plans and goals so quickly? You're excited about his commitment to the Lord and his desire to become more actively involved in Christian service. But you wish he had reviewed this decision with you ahead of time.

When you remind him of yesterday's goals, he resents your intrusion and insists the Lord led him to sign up. He points out that when he made profession of his faith, he pledged to give Christ first place in his life and to worry less about academic and financial success. "So what's the big deal?" he asks.

The Adolescent's World

In each of these situations we see signs of tension between a parent's preference for long-range planning and a teenager's interest in solving today's problems today. The teenagers' decisions make sense in their world: Alan is having fun. Jenna is able to spend more time with Tom. And Michael wants to put his faith into action. But, as parents, we may find it difficult to understand and accept these decisions. They just don't seem right to us.

We adults invest more time in deliberate planning and careful evaluating than our teenagers do. We emphasize the importance of looking at both the "pros" and the "cons" of any new idea before acting on it. Our range of vision is wider. We look at consequences, and we're willing to postpone or drop plans if necessary. So we're not just surprised at these impulsive behaviors . . . we're troubled by them, and they often become the occasion for some fairly strong conflict. Power struggles emerge. It feels as if we and our teens live in separate worlds.

As we reflect on these impulsive behaviors, it's important for us to remember that they do not arise in a vacuum. In real life, these sudden new ideas, changes of belief, and impulsive actions seem very unforeseeable to us. But, like earthquakes on a fault-line, these unpredictable moments are really quite predictable when we remember what's going on in an adolescent's world.

Teens are gaining control over an expanding world

Teenagers are discovering that the house they live in has many more rooms than they ever imagined. Their physical development gives them the ability and stamina to tackle experiences that they only dreamed about when they were ten years old. Their group of friends is expanding, and they are becoming familiar with parts of town other than their own. Access to a set of wheels opens all kinds of doors to adventure and new experiences.

A major milestone on the journey to independence is the first paycheck. Money is a form of power. A teenager who earns $20 per week has new access to food, fuel, entertainment, and drugs. Given some cash and a car, teenagers quickly move from a rather limited and predictable world of choices to one in which they face an amazing array of new options.

Teens are discovering their place in this expanding world

An adolescent's growing awareness of this bigger world may be expressed through an interest in watching the news on TV and reading the newspaper. He or she may surprise you by becoming concerned about a current political issue or by participating in a protest march focusing on an environmental issue.

Often teens become frustrated and impatient with others, and perhaps with themselves, for having spent so much time, money, and energy on the shrunken world of self. This sense of idealism leads them to become critical of their past and open to bold expressions of personal involvement in global issues as they face their future.

Teens frequently develop a new appreciation for persons from racial, cultural, and religious backgrounds different from their own.

They forge into this new arena of *the foreign* with the zeal of a cheerleader, celebrating the removal of barriers and cherishing the opportunity to demonstrate unconditional love and acceptance to strangers.

Teens focus on friendships

Since emancipation from parents is such a major developmental task for all teenagers, peer friendships gain increasing importance during these years. As teens experiment with distancing themselves from parents and family, they often feel separated and alone. To offset this painful feeling, they go out of their way to secure friendships with peers.

Because teens sometimes feel guilty for separating themselves from parental influence and control, they find it comforting to discover that their peers are experiencing similar struggles. In times of conflict with parents, teens often believe they are the cause of all this pain and consequently judge themselves unlovable. When accepting, affirming peers come to the rescue as friends, teens are once again assured of their worth.

Maintaining friends, then, is crucial in adolescent development. Any hint of being overlooked or rejected by peers can be devastating. To gain acceptance, teens will often uncritically accept their friends' suggestions as normative and act in ways that we consider impulsive. When reacting to their actions, we should remember the enormous power peer pressure has on a teen's decision making.

Teens seek a faith that works

Teenagers do not disregard the need to understand and clarify their religious beliefs and will often invest considerable time in discussion and debate in order to clarify their own personal beliefs. There may be times when they defend beliefs quite contrary to those you have taught them, thus putting family values to the test.

Studies repeatedly show that teenagers respond most positively to a relevant religious faith. They seek a faith system that is connected to real-life issues and experiences. Teens are becoming alert to the needs and hurts of neighbors around the corner and around the globe, and they really want to make a difference in their world. As a result, parents of teens often encounter a flood of criticism levied against boring preachers and lazy church members who never do anything to show that they are really Christians.

Teens may threaten to abandon ship and drop out of church life completely as part of their campaign to change their world. They often make impulsive commitments of time, money, and personal energy to translate their words into works of love.

Teens remember the spontaneity of their childhood

Parents smile at the spontaneity of an eight-year-old who dares to giggle, laugh, dance, weep, or cheer without inhibition. We celebrate this childish freedom to express feelings and to act spontaneously.

But sometimes we forget that teenagers are still close enough to their own childhood to remember how to have fun. Some of their impulsive behavior may simply indicate their sense of freedom to openly experience moments of pleasure as well as pain. Perhaps we should celebrate these reminders that our teens are alive, alert, and well!

Teens may prefer to resist rather than to surrender

Sometimes our teenagers' impulsive behavior may be an expression of subtle resistance or even of outright defiance. For example, Alan's midnight swim at the gravel pit could well be his way of testing the limits or of letting you know he is no longer willing to accept your rules as norms in his life. What appears to be an impulsive, spur-of-the-moment decision may really be just the tip of the iceberg. Alan could be making his declaration of independence. His midnight foray into independent living may serve as a clear signal that he thinks of himself no longer as a child but as a young adult. He's claiming new turf and is keenly interested in observing your response to his challenge.

Keeping in Touch Can Be Costly

Your daughter Julie has been dating Greg for about a year, and you feel pretty good about the relationship. It's meant a lot to Julie to know that Greg thinks the world of her. That's why she was so crushed when he told her he and his family would be spending the summer in Boston, caring for his grandparents. Four days after Greg leaves, you find out that Julie has been calling him every afternoon. Each conversation lasted more than half an hour! You simply cannot afford to pay such huge Denver-to-Boston phone bills, and you're troubled by the fact that Julie has made these calls without asking your permission. When you ask her for an explanation, the only reason she can give is that she misses him so much. "I just had to keep in touch!" she insists.

How do you respond? Parents certainly have the right to set limits on long-distance phone calls, especially when they're paying the bills. If Julie had been willing to share with you her longing to talk with Greg, you might have discussed the cost with her. You might have agreed to allow her to place time-limited calls once or twice a week when the rates are lowest. Or you might have encouraged her to start writing letters as an alternative way of keeping in touch. It's the impulsiveness of her decision that makes it difficult for you to get beyond your irritation and, perhaps, your anger.

Examples like this remind us of how focused adolescents can be on the *now* of their experience. In response to her feelings of loneliness and her deep desire to maintain contact with Greg, Julie simply sees no other alternative than the phone calls. She has compartmentalized her world. Financial principles that she might use in another compartment do not seem valid here. She needs to talk with Greg—now!

We've already suggested that decisions like this usually express an adolescent's growing need to be accepted and affirmed by peers. This is certainly true for Julie, who has fallen madly in love with her first "real" boyfriend. *What* they discuss is relatively insignificant, but *that* they keep talking has become extremely important.

Your reaction to her costly calls will probably become the occasion for some intense conversation, some raised voices, and perhaps even some tears. Julie will consider your constant concern about cost to be highly insensitive, selfish, and unloving. "You just don't know how important it is for Greg and me to stay close! We're really in love, and when people are in love, they talk about everything!" she might exclaim.

Now let's suppose that the day after this disagreement, Julie's youth group leader from church calls to ask her to sign up for the retreat scheduled for next month. It will cost twenty dollars. She declines, saying it's too expensive. You're tempted to challenge her on the inconsistency of her response. She has just confronted *you* on your unwillingness to generously cover the costs of her phone calls, yet *she* refuses to participate in a church function because she's saving her money for a new coat. From your perspective the inconsistency is blatant.

But not so for Julie. She will defend both her right to keep in touch with Greg at great cost and her decision to decline the invitation to attend the retreat. There may be other reasons leading her to decline the invitation, but the issue she identifies is the cost. For Julie, only two things matter—Greg and a new coat. Attending the retreat with kids she doesn't particularly like (at this time) is not on her priority list. In evidence in Julie's attitude—and in the lives of many adolescents—is a kind of social pragmatism that gives highest importance to one issue: "How can I keep my best friends?"

In situations like this it is most helpful if parents, recognizing their teen's self-centeredness, respond with patience and understanding. It would not be appropriate or helpful to harshly criticize Julie for her inconsistency or to call her a hypocrite. However, when tempers have cooled, and you have occasion to reflect on the entire situation with her in a more relaxed way, you could begin by assuring her that you are trying to understand her reasons for arriving at her decisions in the way she did. She needs that affirmation from you. You should also honestly share with her your concern about how these two decisions conflict with each other. She needs guidance on how to move beyond impulsive decisions focused narrowly on her own present needs to a more reflective approach that takes in a bigger picture.

In my work with adolescents, I've found it helpful to suggest the simple grid "Stop. Think. Act." as a useful guide for teens in making decisions. They often acknowledge the usefulness of this grid in moving beyond a narrow, impulsive world to a broader, inclusive world of considerations. The long-term effect of this kind of counsel is that you are in fact coaching them into the adult world of responsible decision making. You are encouraging emancipation by challenging them to look at the bigger picture.

Listen to the Thunder

We've been looking at behaviors that move directly from the heart to the hands, short-circuiting the head. Impulsive behavior is a response to a whim, a feeling, or a conviction. It involves minimal reflection and review. Scripture frequently warns us about the dangers of such unthinking behavior.

One of the major marks of maturity is a person's ability to think before speaking and acting. Adolescents are living between two worlds. They are leaving the world of childhood, in which one's thinking is focused on the familiar, the local, and the personal. But many of them have not yet fully entered the world of adulthood, in which one's thinking looks beyond one's own turf and one's own agenda to the world of others—not only locally but also globally.

So the fact that teens specialize in rash behavior should come as no surprise to us. They become impatient to establish their own identity as independent persons, and their idealism fuels their passion to change their world. This impatience and idealism may contribute to the "accidental selfishness" of their impulsive behavior. They do not intend to be selfish but often fall into that trap by virtue of their failure to seek insight from others before deciding and doing.

Usually their behavior is not a matter for serious concern. But sometimes we must listen more carefully to the thunder. When impulsive behavior becomes the pattern, when it brings harm to the teenager or to others, and when it leads to violation of the law, we must seriously address this problem. Examples of out-of-control behavior might include forays of compulsive spending, intense outbursts of temper in response to relatively minor incidents, storming out of the house when confronted, running away from home, borrowing another's property without permission, spurts of generosity leading to excessive giving, shoplifting, heavy use of alcohol and drugs, eating disorders, and suicidal gestures. Obviously these behaviors all deserve careful attention from parents—and perhaps a pastor or a professional counselor as well.

Watch Out, World . . . Here We Come!

Adolescents are not adults. Their world is different from ours.

Given their need for acceptance by friends, they place high priority on conformity. They want to dress as their friends do, no matter what we say. (Incidentally, they really don't want us to dress like them!) Their idealism gives them courage to challenge the status quo, whether in the home, school, church, community, or world. Their commitments can be strong, compelling, and beautiful.

I think it's important for us to be reflective rather than impulsive in our response to their intensity. As models of maturity, we should respond with patience and understanding when faced with the surprises they spring on us. We should be able to step back from the immediate situation and place the event in the context of the bigger picture. After all, Alan did survive his midnight swim. Jenna will graduate without that honors English course. And, in spite of five weeks of lost wages, Michael will still be able to attend college. While encouraging them to think responsibly before deciding and doing, we should also affirm them for their efforts to cope, as they grow into adulthood.

Jesus encourages us to look behind the "motions" to the motives, as he did. When the woman anointed his feet at the home of Simon in Bethany (Mark 14:1-9), Jesus did not support the critics of extravagance. Instead he blessed the woman for her impulsive display of love, described it as a beautiful thing, and even used it as an opportunity to offer instruction about his forthcoming death.

I enjoy the story of a boy who was forced to join his parents in attending a reception for the great concert pianist Paderewski. Bored with the formality of it all, the boy impulsively seated himself at the concert piano and began playing his favorite song, "Chopsticks." Paderewski took note of the situation and immediately moved toward the piano, seating himself next to the boy. He began accompanying the boy, adding rich and colorful themes to the notes the boy was hammering out. And he whispered in the boy's ear, "Keep playing!"

Let's be thankful our teens are in there . . . alive and kicking. They have not yet arrived. Nor have we. By God's grace, we may see a bigger picture than they do, but we join them in the challenging task of moving from the narrow world of self to the broader world of others. As we travel together, we should lean over and whisper "Keep playing!" as a promise of our loving partnership with them in the school of discipleship under Christ.

Suggestions for Group Session

Getting Started
In the first chapter we identified open communication as an essential ingredient of healthy family life. In this chapter we're dealing with the impulsive behavior of teens and with the tense situations such behavior can create in the family. We'll see that the way we respond to our teens' behavior may either create communication breakdowns or contribute to deeper levels of understanding and love.

Scripture Readings
1 Corinthians 13:4-7: After reading this passage, spend a few minutes identifying guidelines for parenting that you find here. Focus on the theme of patience as expressed in the phrase, "Love never gives up."

Opening Prayer
Pray that God will help each of you grow in patience and in the ability to show solid love and support to your teens.

Additional Scriptures for Your Review
Matthew 4:8-20: Note Simon and Andrew's radical (impulsive?) decisions to quit their jobs and follow Jesus.
Mark 2:1-5: Note the impatience (impulsiveness?) of the four friends who damage a neighbor's roof in order to meet their goal.
Matthew 8:18-22 and Luke 14:25-33: Compare these two passages. How do you explain Jesus' teachings in these passages? On the one hand he expects radical surrender. Yet he also asserts that we should calculate the cost before surrendering to him.

For Discussion
What Would You Do?

1. Take another look at the real-life "shockers" listed at the beginning of this chapter:
   - *Sara* registers with a cult group.
   - *Kevin* gets his ear pierced.
   - *Jane* plans a spring-break trip.
   - *Steve* drops out of the school choir.

29

One way to generate helpful discussion is to role-play these situations. Try to simulate the debate that would emerge between parents and teens in each of these situations. Then discuss your reactions and share suggestions about how you would respond if this were to happen in your family. Would you give a green, yellow, or red light to these behaviors? Defend your choices.

2. React and respond to the following quotes. What implications do each of them have for the parents of teens?

"I really feel empty inside. I think I'm just a social box. I'm not really sure of who I am, because I just go along with the group, no matter what they say. I'm so empty, it scares me to death!"

—A lonely teenage girl

"The thirteenth and fourteenth years commonly are the most difficult twenty-four months in life. It is during this time that self-doubt and feelings of inferiority reach an all-time high, amidst the greatest social pressures yet experienced. An adolescent's worth as a human being hangs precariously on peer group acceptance, which is notoriously fickle. Thus, relatively minor evidences of rejection or ridicule are of major significance to those who already see themselves as fools and failures."
—*From* The Strong-Willed Child, *James Dobson; pp. 190-191*

"My parents are cool. They know I do some really dumb stuff, but they give me lots of space. I know when they think I've blown it, but they just let me learn by my own mistakes.
—A vibrant teenage boy

Why Do Teenagers Sometimes Behave Impulsively?

3. The following reasons are frequently offered as explanations of impulsive behavior in adolescents:
   - Fear of facing consequences for disobedience
   - Fear of being overlooked or belittled by peers
   - Fear of being abandoned by a boyfriend or girlfriend
   - Desire for increasing independence
   - Curiosity
   - Compartmentalization (a narrow, single-issue line of vision)
   - Impatience with adults' patience (refusal to accept the status quo)

- Possibility thinking that dares to ask, "What if?" (idealism)
- A faulty notion of personal invincibility
- The need to prove one's sexual identity

Select the two or three items from this list that you consider to be the most common explanations of adolescent impulsivity. Defend your choices, giving examples from your own experience, if possible. Which of these apply to the experiences of Alan, Jenna, Michael, and Julie, described earlier in this chapter? Can you add other reasons to this list?

Closing

Review the guidelines for parents listed below, talking about some of their implications for your parenting. Then close your session in prayer, asking for God's wisdom as you deal with your often impulsive and unpredictable teens. You may wish to close your prayer by singing "Lord, Listen to Your Children Praying" (*Psalter Hymnal* 625), a reminder that before God both we and our teens are children in need of our holy parent's love and care.

Guidelines for Parents

- *Keep up with your teens*

Like summer showers in Florida and earthquakes in California, unpredictable behavior is quite predictable for most adolescents. As Christian parents, we should observe and attempt to understand what's going on in their lives. Sharing some of your family experiences with other parents can be very helpful. Also, be sure to take advantage of the growing number of books written for parents that may help you to better understand the dynamics of adolescent development. Our teens are on a journey, and the scenery is constantly changing!

- *Be honestly shocked*

Your teens need to know your reactions to their decisions and actions. In responding to their questionable and unacceptable decisions, it is important that you share your questions, fears, disappointment, and anger with them. Help them see that your interest in these matters is intended as an expression of your unconditional love for them. They must hear over and over again that you want the best for them!

- *Be compassionate in your critique*

In our evaluation of our teenagers' impulsivity we must always strive to "walk in their shoes" before rendering a verdict. We must seek to understand their feelings and look at life from their perspective. Compassion reminds us that young adults are still *young* adults! Compassion also leads us to humbly acknowledge our own excursions into impulsivity. Perhaps some parental examples of the problems created by our own failure to stop, think, and act would be helpful. And we should remember that love keeps no record of wrongs.

- *Be a good waiter*
  In light of God's never-failing forgiveness and the Spirit's tireless work in sanctification, we should pray for unending patience and long-suffering. We yearn for the "quick fix" and for instant maturity. But life is a pilgrimage, and holiness comes slowly. We should not excuse our teens from accepting the consequences of their own decisions. They are accountable for their own actions. (For example, Julie should eventually pay for her phone calls.)

  In this long-term process, our teens will join us in the lifelong school of discipleship at the feet of the One who calls us to serve him with reckless abandon.

THREE

Fights Over Fairness

Josh is seven years old. He just stormed off to his room because you insisted that he sweep the garage before he goes out to play. "My friends don't have to do so much work around the house!" he exclaims. "You're just not fair!"

Josh is ten years old. He just stormed off to his room because you've rejected his request to drop piano lessons and told him that he should continue for at least another year. "You let Julie quit her lessons last year. If my sister doesn't have to take lessons, why should I?" he asks. "You're just not fair!"

Josh is fifteen years old. He just stormed off to his room because you informed him you would not permit him to join his two buddies for a five-day unchaperoned campout. "Eric and Alan's parents trust them. Fifteen-year-olds should be allowed to be on their own once in a while!" he insists. "You're just not fair!"

Josh is eighteen years old. He just stormed off to his room because you told him that he wouldn't be allowed to host the spring-break trip to Florida in your new van. "You let Julie use the van all the time!" he complains. "You're just not fair!"

Listen to Josh's Lament

Josh has a hunch. He believes in the principle of fairness. He believes that if he is treated a certain way in one situation, he should be treated in a similar way in other situations. Or he may insist that if Julie has been granted certain privileges, then he has a

33

right to expect the same favors. Or he may argue that if his uncle, or his neighbor, or his best friend's parents give certain privileges to their kids, then you should be willing to offer the same benefits to him. He sometimes wonders why the God who does so many nice things for others seems to be giving him so many problems and difficulties to deal with.

What Josh is doing is comparing his own present situation with similar situations in his past or in the lives of others. He assumes that life should be consistent and dependable. In his quest for security, he assumes that there are some things he should be able to count on.

When parents frequently change their minds, tighten a teen's restrictions and penalties, or handle similar situations differently than other parents do, they will undoubtedly be labeled "unfair" by their adolescents. God is sometimes judged unfair too. After all, why does God permit some people to be so rich, so healthy, and so successful, while others have such a tough time in life? Josh the teenager believes deeply that life ought to be fair.

A Major Issue for Teens

Many factors make fairness emerge as a major theme for young people. As teenagers move toward independence, they focus much of their energy on clarifying their sense of personal identity. They wonder about their worth. Whenever they feel they are being overlooked or mistreated, their sense of self-esteem is challenged. Their complaints about unfair treatment may be their necessary defense against what they perceive to be uncaring attacks upon their fragile ego at a time when they crave affirmation and approval.

An essential component in the shift from childhood to adulthood is the world of expanding relationships. Secure children are prepared to take the risk of forming a broader range of attachments in adolescence. These peer friendships are strengthened by hours of intense conversation at school and over the phone and by visits to one another's homes.

It should come as no surprise that teens will make comparisons as they become familiar with other family patterns. Because they trust your love, they dare to challenge your decisions in the light of these alternative models they are observing in the homes of their friends. Indeed, as teens mature, they become increasingly analytical and critical of their personal and family experiences. In the shift from asking "What is?" to the bolder question "What if?" they will undoubtedly question parents on a wide range of topics. This growing commitment to insist on global principles of justice and fairness equips idealistic teenagers to press for cosmic compliance. And where do they begin? Right in their own homes!

Adolescents often live with clear-cut categories of right and wrong, good and evil, fair and unfair. Their concern for principles should be applauded. Seeking to put the principle of fairness into practice, however, should be an ongoing process in every family. Fairness should be both firm and flexible—which makes it a primary item for discussion and review between parents and teens.

Fighting for Fairness

Parents and children deal with questions of fairness every day. Younger children raise the question when you're distributing candy or chicken legs, when you're making decisions about who helps with the dishes and who chooses the next TV program. So it's important to remember that our teens' fights for fairness are a continuation of a theme that has been important for them since early childhood. Teens, however, seem to put this issue on center stage.

Let's look at a number of examples of how fairness often becomes the occasion for conflict between parents and teens.

Privileges

- June, your sixteen-year-old daughter, complains about her limited telephone privileges. She reminds you in strong terms about how unfair it is that she can only make two ten-minute phone calls per night, while her eighteen-year-old brother has no limits at all on his calls.

- Ted, your fourteen-year-old firstborn son, is basically an easygoing kid, but he is really critical of you for allowing his younger brother and sister to watch more TV and to stay up a lot later than he ever could. "When I was their age, you were a lot more strict with me!" he laments.

- Alycia, seventeen, labels you as tyrants because of the way you monitor her dating habits. She's convinced that her sixteen-year-old sister doesn't have to tell you a thing about the guy or the group she's going out with. "It's just not fair that you trust her and don't give me any freedom to make my own decisions!" she exclaims.

It seems everything parents do in managing the family comes under careful review. Your decisions about allowances, TV, telephones, study time, chores, curfews, use of the good car, and entertainment are all scrutinized by teenagers armed with the principles of "fairness, freedom, and justice for all"! Adolescents often protest what they judge to be an unfair distribution of wealth—whether in the form of food, finances, or freedoms.

35

Penalties

- Kyle, your fourteen-year-old son, is known for his ability to instantly make any room in your home look as though a tornado just passed through. Your rule of "Straighten up your room and make your bed in the morning, or no TV for the rest of the day" is the only thing that has worked. But lately he's insisting that you drop this unfair penalty. He tells you that his room is his own territory and that his two best friends don't even have to make their beds.

- Justin is incensed at your insistence that he not use the car for a month. He admits that he did break curfew and drank some beer, but he thinks your punishment is wildly unfair and unjust. "You're making a mountain out of a molehill!" he insists.

Most teenagers review their sanctions, limits, and penalties with the scrutiny of a surgeon's eye. In their quest for increasing freedom to make their own decisions, they remind you that earlier punishments are no longer appropriate. They resent penalties that they judge to be "harsh and unusual" in response to minor infractions of your rules. Carefully researched comparisons between your treatment of them and your treatment of other kids in the family, or between your handling of an issue and the way their friends' parents are handling the same issue, are reported with intensity.

Providence

- Jason is fourteen. Since his parents' divorce five years ago, he has been living with his mother, and he often still worries that he might have caused the divorce. Jason is lonely, depressed, and angry at God. "Why should I have to face all these problems?" he asks. "Life just isn't fair!"

- Your sixteen-year-old daughter, Anne, and her boyfriend, Tom, are on their way home from a basketball game. A drunk driver hits them head on. Anne's boyfriend is killed, and Anne sustains serious injuries. She's overwhelmed with grief, bitterness, and resentment. "If God's in control, why did this tragedy happen? Didn't God know what a great person Tom was? The drunk driver is the one who should have been killed!" she asserts.

Teens often struggle with the correlation between God's sovereignty and our human responsibility. When tragedy strikes a member of their family or friendship circle, they often raise a long list of questions:

"Why did God do this to her?"

"Why did God let this senseless tragedy happen?"

"Why doesn't God intervene?"

They are also becoming aware of the bigger world beyond the confines of family and friends. Adolescents demonstrate increased concern over the plight of the unemployed, the hungry, the homeless, and the oppressed in their "global village." Because of inequities they discern in the worldwide distribution of privileges and provisions, teens are quick to challenge God's sense of justice and fairness.

Are We Sometimes Unfair?

It's important for us as parents to reflect on the situations that lead teenagers to criticize us for unfairness. Perhaps sometimes we *do* disregard the principle of fairness without even realizing it.

Do some of these observations sound familiar to you?

1. "Talk about unfair! Around our house you never know what will happen when you get into trouble. If Mom or Dad is in a bad mood, watch out! They really lay it on heavy!"

Parents sometimes assign penalties for misbehavior on the basis of their feelings of frustration, disappointment, anger, or sadness. Although these feelings may be appropriate and need to be expressed, we should avoid letting them influence the type and severity of punishment we administer. Exaggerated criticisms and excessive penalties will often "provoke [our] children to anger" (Eph. 6:4, RSV) and deserve to be labeled as unfair.

2. "Talk about unfair! They're still treating me like a ten- year-old!"

Well, are we? Perhaps we need to review some of the rules and limits we use with our adolescents in the light of their appropriate desire to exercise increasing responsibility for their own decisions and actions.

3. "Talk about unfair! How can I show my parents that I am trustworthy when they never give me the space to prove it?"

Hidden behind this complaint is a challenge to us. As Christian parents we need to trust the Lord to bless the efforts we've put forth in training our children to live as Christians. Our deep love for our kids may fill us with fear when we think of the things that can go wrong, but we simply must give our teens increasing opportunity to put their Christian training into practice. Adolescents need space to succeed—which means we must allow them space to fail, as well.

4. "Talk about unfair! I'm really sick of getting mixed messages from my parents. Dad says one thing, and Mom comes up with some-

37

thing completely different. It's like they don't even touch base with each other before giving me the verdict!"

Teens may become experts at playing one parent off the other. They find this "splitting" particularly effective when they sense that their parents seldom discuss their ideas together before arriving at a decision. Often one parent tends to minimize or overlook issues, while the other acts as the watchdog and enforcer.

Although this problem occurs in many two-parent families, it is even more prevalent in situations where parents are separated or divorced. In some cases, the noncustodial parent may join his or her visiting teen in criticizing the custodial parent for being unduly harsh. Whenever separated parents are involved in setting rules and limits, it is essential that they agree on the ground rules and enforce them in a similar fashion.

5. "Talk about unfair! Our entire history class was goofing off. I'm the only one who couldn't go to the class party because we messed up!"

Although we, as parents, have the right and the responsibility to make decisions we judge to be appropriate in rearing our children, it's important for us to take into consideration the way other families handle similar situations. Our teens will become bitter and resentful if they are subjected to penalties that clearly exceed those assigned to their friends.

6. "Talk about unfair! It won't do me any good to explain to my father that I kept asking the driver of our group to take me home. Some of the kids I was with smoked pot, and I got home late. My dad smelled the pot and really laid into me. There's no changing his mind—even if my friends tell him I didn't smoke it."

This angry teen resents not only his dad's impulsive response but also his dad's unwillingness to hear the whole story. In some cases our children may in fact be struggling to honor the principles we endorse as they carve out their niche with peers. They need our sympathetic understanding and a listening ear as we ponder the problems that sometimes arise. New facts may lead us to modify our earlier decisions. Changing one's mind in a situation like this is not weakness but strength!

7. "Talk about unfair! My parents really box me in with rules. They keep telling me I have to be a good example for the younger kids in the family."

It might be helpful to reflect on the impact of birth order in our parenting decisions. Do we expect more from the oldest child in the family? If we modify our expectations for younger children, do we

38

adequately explain our reasons for these changes to the older kids? Do we indulge our youngest child as a way to offset some of the guilt feelings we may carry because we think we weren't generous and kind enough to our older children?

8. "Talk about unfair! I really hate being a twin. I'm supposed to think, feel, dress, and act exactly like my sister. We're not identical, no matter what the doctor said!"

Twins sometimes resent the expectations that parents, relatives, and friends may unconsciously lay on them to measure up to their mates. Every person is given unique interests and talents by the Lord. Parents are called to cultivate these gifted persons as unique individuals—without favoring one over the other. Expressing fairness in parenting twins offers unique challenges.

9. "Talk about unfair! My dad runs our home like a police state! I can't even sneeze without getting his permission!"

As our children move into adolescence, our fear as parents may lead us to focus less on community and caring and more on control. This need to control may spring from the baggage we carry with us from our own upbringing. In some cases, extreme parental strictness simply mirrors the way parents were raised themselves. Unfortunately, children who were victims of tyrannical parents may become parents who unwittingly work out their unresolved anger by victimizing their own children.

Fairness: A Good Way to Show Love

Fairness issues deserve our ongoing attention—especially as our adolescents move toward adulthood. Our teens need to be assured, over and over again, that they may claim their God-given right to stand up and be counted as independent persons with unique personal identities. Their call for fairness may well be a request to have their personal rights and dignity honored at a crucial time in their development.

But it is also more than that. Teens are searching for assurance that there are some abiding principles by which they can understand and manage their expanding world. They need to participate in the family struggle to honor fairness as a dependable, working principle for the ordering of their lives. If we model fairness in a loving way with them, they will be better equipped to move toward the kind of spiritual maturity that encourages them to blend justice and love in their dealings with others.

Fairness is usually marked by a sense of consistency and predictability—but not always! Fairness pays close attention to the uniqueness of each person and the uniqueness of each new situation. Fairness goes beyond enforcing the rules to consistently expressing the rule of love. And love bends. Love listens. Love learns. For example, breaking curfew may be a violation of family rules. One son may come home late and be penalized. But if another son comes home late and explains that he helped a stranded motorist change a tire, you will respond not with penalties but with praise. This kind of inconsistency is not unfair, but loving and just.

Fairness always assumes some point of comparison. It demands that we compare with other models our present decisions to give, to withhold, to penalize, or to allow. We may refer back to how we handled a similar situation in the past. We may compare a current situation with how we treat other children in our family. We may take into account how other families handle similar situations. We may compare our plans with the way parents' and childrens' rights and responsibilities are defined by the laws of our land. And, of course, we search for guiding principles through Scripture reading and prayer as we chart our course as parents.

All of this takes conscientious effort and ongoing work. It's not only appropriate but also essential for parents and teenagers to place discussion of fairness issues high on their agenda. Teens need to hear from us that we expect them to treat us fairly. And they need to hear us pledge that, with God's help, we will honor the principle of fairness in our dealings with them and with the other children in our family.

Achieving fairness in the family often involves struggle. When teens feel their rights have been violated, they demand justice. When parents feel their expectations have been disregarded, they, too, demand justice. Often teens who violate family rules seem to be challenging their parents' authority. In doing so, they threaten their parents' perceived role, and the parents sometimes start viewing the teens as enemies. Hostile feelings displace loving listening, and conflict escalates.

Loving parents must always be willing to sit down with teenagers and review family expectations, rules, and consequences. Parents and teens can formulate sanctions and penalties together. Some families spell out such things in the form of a contract. By predicting certain situations ahead of time, they avoid painful encounters. One family, for example, had discussed and agreed upon penalties for reckless driving several months before their son received his first speeding ticket.

Giving appropriate unconditional love in timely ways is always fair. And teenagers who know they are really loved unconditionally are equipped to cooperate and to celebrate the generous love you show not only to them but also to other members of the family. Love is always fair!

Suggestions for Group Session

Getting Started

In this chapter we're dealing with a topic that usually brings parents and teens into some fairly intense conflict. Teens often raise the subject of fairness as a strong protest. Parents often feel personally criticized when their decisions are challenged by angry adolescents. It's painful for parents who think they are being fair to be told in no uncertain terms that they are unfair tyrants! The subject deserves our careful attention.

Opening Prayer

Thank God for your teens and ask the God of justice to help you deal fairly and justly and lovingly with your children.

Scripture Readings

Genesis 25:19-34: Reflect on the dangerous alliances here between Isaac and Esau, Rebekah and Jacob. Look for illustrations of unfairness in the unfolding family drama.

Matthew 20:1-16: In Jesus' parable of the workers in the vineyard, how does generous love inform our thinking about fairness? Does love go beyond fairness?

Psalm 73:12-14: Consider the lament offered in these verses. Discuss the permission God gives us to raise "fairness" questions. How is the issue resolved for Asaph?

For Discussion

When Do You Fight About Fairness?

1. In this chapter we address a wide range of situations in which teens challenge their parents' fairness. Review the list of issues raised in the opening section of this chapter:
   - Privileges

     June—phone restrictions

     Ted—TV time

     Alycia—freedom to choose her own friends and dating partners
   - Penalties

     Kyle—punishments for a messy room

     Justin—driving restriction because of drinking
   - Providence

     Jason—complaints because of loss of stable family life

     Anne—complaints related to death of boyfriend at the hand of a drunken driver

Identify and share examples in each of these categories that have emerged as difficult issues for your family. Select a few issues that seem to hit home for most of you and role-play a heated conversation between a parent and a teen, demonstrating the strong opinions on both sides and the way these issues can be resolved peacefully.

Some Common Complaints

2. The section *"Are* We Sometimes Unfair?" presents some of the more common complaints raised by adolescents about parents.

   a. they assign punishments when they are angry.

   b. they refuse to modify rules from earlier years.

   c. they refuse to give teens increasing freedom to make their own decisions.

   d. one of them is strict and the other is lenient.

   e. they assign heavier punishments than siblings or friends receive for similar infractions.

   f. they seem unwilling to hear their teen's side of the story.

   g. they overemphasize using older children as an example for younger children.

   h. they expect identical twins to think, feel, and act in identical ways.

   i. they are perceived as being strict, rigid, and unbending in their ideas.

   Spend some time discussing this list in small groups. Describe situations in your family which suggest that at times these criticisms might be valid. How can you tell the difference between a teenager's genuine concern for defending the principle of fairness and his or her tendency to sometimes use the argument of fairness to protect selfish interests? Identify situations in which a teen's call for fairness might not be valid.

Other Fairness Issues

3. As indicated earlier, adolescents often question God's fairness when they encounter inequity and tragedy. Anne's anger at God for the untimely death of her boyfriend and for her loss of physical health led her to criticize God as unloving, unfair, and unbelievable. *Is* life unfair? How could you encourage Anne to renew her faith in God?

4. A family with four children, including two teenagers, often argued about who should choose the music to be played on the

family stereo. The father proposed a simple rule: Any member of the family may play his or her music if no one else is already doing so. Family members were encouraged to try to appreciate one another's musical selections. The father maintained that this rule encouraged fairness and mutual consideration by all family members. Do you agree? Would such a rule work in your family? Explain.

5. "It's not unusual for us to give more freedom to our more responsible fifteen-year-old son than to our less responsible sixteen-year-old son!" Does this statement honor or disregard the principle of fairness? Explain.

Closing

After each of you jots down one or two resolutions that will help you and your teens work toward a greater degree of loving fairness in the weeks to come, pray silently, asking God to help you keep your resolutions and to grow in your ability to show unconditional love to your children.

FOUR

WHEN FAMILY TIES NO LONGER BIND

Your son Jonathan is really excited. His friend Brian just called to invite him to join their family for supper on Friday and then go with them to the opening football game of the season. You initially share his excitement, but when you check the family calendar, you detect a major conflict.

"Jonathan, this week Friday is Grandma's birthday!" you explain. "She invited us a few weeks ago already to go out for dinner with her that night. You know we've always celebrated her birthday with her."

The tension mounts as Jonathan pleads his case. He insists on his right to accept Brian's invitation to go to the game. It's the season opener, and he's so proud to have been invited by Brian and his family to join them. "Besides," he reminds you, "I'm so bored at those family get-togethers. All my cousins are much younger than me, and Grandma just talks with all you older people anyway!"

Jonathan's dilemma may remind you of some of the situations that develop in your home. We all have good memories of those days when our families felt really close—days when our kids seemed to be elated to be doing lots of things with each other . . . and with Mom and Dad as well. On our best days, this familiar hymn really seemed to fit:

Blest be the tie that binds
our hearts in Christian love;

45

the fellowship of kindred minds
is like to that above.

If only family life could always be like that! We yearn for those times when we felt close—parents with children . . . brothers and sisters all enjoying each other's company. We thank the Lord for the times when family life really feels good.

But if we listen closely as our children slip into adolescence, we can often hear rumbles of thunder in the distance. In this chapter we will take a look at the way family ties seem to fall apart when our children reach their teen years.

Stormy Days Ahead!

Ever since you put up the backboard in your driveway two years ago, your fourteen-year-old son Jack has really enjoyed having his twelve-year-old brother Ricky join him for hoops. The two of them have spent hours together every day after school practicing their shots. In fact, your driveway has become the "place to be" in the neighborhood.

But lately things have been different. Jack and his three friends are all hoping to make the JV team at school next month, so they are getting serious about their game. Ricky complains that Jack no longer wants him around—and it seems to be true. Ricky loves basketball, and he also thinks the world of his older brother, but Jack no longer seems to have time for a twelve-year-old. He tells Ricky not to bother them—that he can use the backboard when the older guys are through with their practice session.

You're dismayed by what you see. Why isn't basketball working anymore as the glue that keeps Jack and Ricky together as friends?

Why? Because things in Jack's world are changing rapidly. Making friends is a major issue for him, and making the team has become his all-encompassing objective in life. Ricky is still convinced that his older brother will always be his best friend, but to Jack, this "family tie" with Ricky now seems like more of a bind than a blessing.

Perhaps if Jack could put labels on his feelings, he'd be willing to admit that it's not that he loves Ricky less. He's just starting to think of "family" in broader terms now. His loyalties are expanding, shifting from family to friends.

As parents we may mourn this shift. After all, Ricky certainly feels rejected. But Jack is on a roll! His world is expanding, and at times it feels as if his family ties no longer bind.

Megan is your fifteen-year-old daughter. Her oldzer brother, Brad, is married and lives in the area. Megan was ecstatic when Brad and his wife had their first child, Timmy, a few months ago. He was your first grandson and Megan's first nephew. All of you were sure Timmy was the most beautiful baby to ever arrive on earth.

During the first weeks after the birth, Megan went to visit the baby constantly, but her commitment to stay close to Timmy soon weakened. She hasn't stopped in to see him for a few weeks now, and she has turned down several invitations to babysit as well. It seems as though she's pulling back from family life.

You're probably right! Megan's devotion to the baby seemed so natural and right at first. But as Megan got back into her school activities, she found less time for Brad and Timmy. (Could it be, too, that she felt squeezed out by all the attention Grandpa and Grandma are giving to Timmy and his parents?) You want Megan to stay close to Timmy, and she assures you that she will. But right now there are other boys who seem more important in her life. At times like this it feels as if your family ties no longer bind.

It's Thursday suppertime. The two of you, Mom and Dad, sit down to eat a meal big enough to feed your family of four.

Just a few minutes ago your daughter called from work to let you know she was asked to stay on until the 9 P.M. closing at the store; she says she'll just grab a bite to eat at the mall. And your son called from his friend's house to let you know he would be eating there and returning to school for band practice. You sit at the table recalling the good times you used to have when the four of you enjoyed breakfast and dinner together every day.

Mealtimes have always been a significant part of your family life—times to catch up on one another's activities. You knew things would change, but you really resent the rather sudden erosion of this tradition of eating together as a family.

It feels as if you're caught in a bind. On the one hand, you want very much to retain the pattern of family mealtimes, because these times have been rewarding for all of you in the past. On the other hand, you're pleased that your teenagers are involved in part-time work, school projects, and social activities. On a night like this you just get the feeling that your family ties no longer bind . . .

The Strains of Pain

The situations described above seem to be quite predictable for families with teenage children. Sometimes, however, the apparent breakdown of family cohesiveness is given added impetus by unfortunate and inappropriate situations at home. Children who question their parents' love for each other and for them will come to associate life at home with anxiety, uneasiness, and pain.

Such children often escape by isolating themselves in their rooms or by hiding in the unreal world of television or in a pleasant fantasy world of their own making. These same children, when entering adolescence, will become more direct in their efforts to escape the anxiety and pain of unsettled life at home. We will consider a number of situations that may create enough pain to nudge teenagers to seek acceptance and support from social networks beyond their own families.

The Pain of Neglect

For those of us who have been blessed with parents who provided appropriate love and nurture throughout our childhood years, it is difficult to understand the pain of children who have been neglected by their parents. Neglect wears many faces. We are all familiar with horrible stories of parents who have been found guilty of criminal negligence because of their failure to cradle their children with basic care and love. We react with indignation when we hear of parents who will allow their children to starve at home while they spend most of their time and money at the bar with their friends. Such neglect is inexcusable!

Children who grow up in such a nurture-deprived environment learn early on to question their parents' love for them. Many teenagers involved in deviant behaviors such as truancy, sexual acting out, and drinking have told me their parents were never there for them when they were younger. These deviant behaviors may be our teenagers' way of testing the waters. By acting out in these obviously unacceptable ways, they are often expressing a deep wish that their parents still demonstrated their love for them by confronting and correcting them for these actions. Or they may do these things as revenge against the parents who failed to give them the love they so desperately needed. Teenagers who remember all the times that their parents were simply not there for them have few good memories of family life. Obviously these children will become the teenagers who couldn't care less about family ties.

But neglect can also be more subtle. Active, dedicated, conscientious parents like ourselves can become so caught up in agendas beyond the homefront that our children may at times also feel the pain of neglect. When we parents invest great amounts of time in our jobs, our sports and recreational activities, our social contacts, and even in church and community involvements, our children will often feel the pain of neglect. We may talk about the quality time we spend with our children, but if our presence becomes the exception rather than the rule, or if we convey a sense that we are not really in tune with our children when they wish to discuss something important with us, they will feel cheated and neglected.

Successful, outgoing, and energetic parents may provide their children with mountains of food, fashionable clothing, impressive gadgets, and memorable vacations, doling out enormous sums of money in the process. However, children are perceptive and discerning. They want our loving *presence* far more than the *presents* we may offer to demonstrate our love.

Teenagers will feel little loyalty to maintaining family ties if they sense they have been an interruption and an impediment to parents whose interests and commitments are really directed beyond the family circle. These adolescents have picked up the message that family ties are not the highest priority in life. In their desire to break away from the family, they may be merely following their leaders.

The Pain of Abuse

It goes without saying that the very idea of child abuse is repulsive to all of us. Our hearts break whenever we learn about children who have been mercilessly abused by uncaring parents. Physical abuse includes overt acts such as hitting, striking, slapping, shoving, pinching, and choking. It also includes depriving children of food, sleep, or basic health care, or abusing them sexually.

Perhaps even more painful, however, are the various forms of psychological and emotional abuse that children endure. These secret sins include a parent's failure to affirm and commend a child, rendering constant criticisms, being unwilling to forgive and forget past mistakes, comparing one child with another, threatening to punish in harsh ways or to abandon a child, or ignoring a child and simply taking him or her for granted.

For Christians, the very thought of abuse is repulsive. We are called not to abuse but to affirm each one of our children. So it is important for us to search our hearts, as parents, to be sure we look upon each one of our children as treasures to be cherished. Each child is a unique work, coming from the hands of the loving Creator, who commissions us to cradle our children with consistent reminders of love and grace. Our children need to know through our love and support that Jesus himself places them on his knee and assures them they will always be part of his family. When children experience overt or subtle abuse within the home, they will have little sense of loyalty to family once they reach their teens. Escape rather than enmeshment will be the order of the day.

The Pain of Strained Family Ties

Another factor that contributes significantly to teenagers' loss of loyalty to family is excessive or unresolved conflict between parents themselves. Most adolescents at risk report deep resentment about what they perceive to be a constant adversarial tone at home. "Whenever I walk through the door at night, I know it's going to be like a civil war in there!" many teens report. When one or the other parent threatens to leave, children are always overcome with a wide array of emotions. In addition to fearing the loss of stable family life, they experience heavy feelings of anger, sadness, hopelessness, depression, and guilt.

Often they believe that if they had been better children, or if they had intervened to rescue the family in a more responsible way, this tragedy could have been averted. These feelings are heightened, of course, when a parent does leave. Separation and divorce shake the very foundations of our childrens' world. Teenagers face complex decisions when their parents separate and divorce. Some become deeply enmeshed with one parent while disowning the other parent as the "culprit." Many teens attempt to maintain appropriate ties with both parents, wanting to avoid choosing sides.

Needless to say, when parents, in their personal quest for peaceful existence, find it necessary to disrupt and at times to terminate a marriage, family life is put on the line. All the members of divorcing families need our understanding, encouragement, and support as they wade through pools of pain.

The Pain of the Empty Chair

Perhaps one of the most confusing and desolating crises that children and young people experience is the death of a sibling or a parent. When family life is good, when relationships are mutually supportive and enriching, and when family life enriches faith and provides fun as well, the death of a family member is simply devastating. As Nicholas Wolterstorff describes poignantly in his book *Lament for a Son* (written after the death of his twenty-five-year-old son Eric), "There's a hole in my world!"

In healthy families it would seem that the initial and long-term impact of such a loss would be to draw the family closer together than ever before. If a father dies, the children and teenagers will naturally rally around their mother by promising their love, support, and assistance. But as time goes on, some young people may become impatient with what they perceive to be their mother's inability or unwillingness to "come to closure" on her mourning. They wish Mother would get on with the business of living. "After all, we're still here with you, Mom!" they say. Mother's mourning may make it very difficult for her to offer the kind of attention her children seek, leaving them with additional feelings of sorrow and abandonment. They may wonder why God seems to be deserting them.

Some teenagers living in this kind of home may become more deeply enmeshed with their mother than ever before. It may become difficult for them to contemplate ever "abandoning" her by leaving home for employment, college, or marriage. Others may find the emotional stresses and strains of home life to be more than they can understand or cope with, leading them to move toward an early departure from the family. For example, they may emotionally invest with renewed compulsion in peer friendships, tying in with their friends' intact families. Or they may move rapidly beyond mere dating relationships to courtship, pursuing early plans for marriage. Such behavior often reflects their deep desire for the restoration of stable family life.

Roots and Wings

It's not bad for teenagers to want to leave home. It's a sign that they're growing up. Christian parents face the daily challenge of providing their children with a secure base on which to stand as well as the courage to assume increasing responsibility for their own lives as they emerge into adulthood. Teenagers often become impatient with our emphasis on roots. They are eager to take off . . . to test their wings. Healthy family life provides both roots and wings.

Some teenagers feel they are *bonded but not bound* by their families. They feel appropriately loved, cherished, and respected by their parents. In families like this, the ties that bind may not seem at all oppressive. Mealtimes continue to be happy, pleasant times in which members of the family report their experiences of the day. Family traditions, such as celebrating grandparents' birthdays and anniversaries, are annual highlights considered too good to be missed. Family vacations are given top priority in everyone's planning.

Teenagers in families like this will still want to move beyond the security of their family circle, but this effort will not be perceived as a breaking away, either by them or by their parents. If this description fits your family, you have much to be thankful for . . . and so do your children.

More often, however, teenagers seem to feel *not only bonded but bound* to their families in ways that lead them to intentionally loosen the ties that bind. Probably for most of us the situations we've reviewed earlier in this chapter come fairly close to home.

This change in family life can be perplexing and painful for adolescents as well as for parents. The routines of shared mealtimes, celebrations, and vacations are no longer cherished. Instead of delivering a satisfying experience of community as they once did, these traditions now create conflict. Our teenagers' growing compulsion to break away from the family circle may begin in low gear, but it often will gain momentum in ways that will become ominous and at times even devastating to our sense of family unity.

If you're experiencing pain because this process is going on in your family, you should not give up hope. Instead you should claim God's covenant promises and remember that even though it may seem as if you're losing your children, the Lord holds them safe in the family of God.

We as parents need to understand that behind our teens' move towards emancipation is an essential and predictable process of maturation. As they ponder the prospect of adult life, adolescents need to ask the basic questions about who they are and what kind of people they want to become. They need to be able to "check themselves out" by moving apart from their family long enough to stand on their own two feet and take a good look. Hopefully they will come to like what they see and will then be able to return to your patient, loving embrace. Their return will bring delight and fulfillment to you as you see your children endorsing their family name, traditions, values, and beliefs for themselves.

While I believe very strongly that the above is true, I also believe that it's valid for parents to establish a set of clear ground rules and expectations for family life. It's good for parents and teens to develop a mutually acceptable general schedule in which a certain number of family meals are planned for each week. Family traditions should be identified and honored. By advance planning, special extended family celebrations can also be plugged into everyone's schedules.

Teenagers need to learn that sacrificing their own preferences for an experience such as a grandparent's birthday is an unavoidable obligation for all families who seek to demonstrate Christian love. Adolescents should also expect to give some of their quality time and interest to their younger brothers and sisters. This is all part of what makes family life rich and rewarding for everyone.

Ground rules such as these can be discussed and clarified through ongoing communication between family members. Of course, exceptions can be granted through negotiation as special situations arise. I believe that a generous, open-minded spirit on the part of parents will generally contribute to a similar attitude on the part of adolescents. Fairness and flexibility will not only foster family cohesiveness but will also prepare our teens for their gradual emergence into the exciting world of adulthood.

Suggestions for Group Session

Getting Started

Family is not something we choose or earn but rather something we are born or adopted into. God intends for this family to embrace its younger members in a love that mirrors God's love for us all. Healthy families should really enjoy life together!

But good families are not excused from strains and pains. Faithful parents often hurt when their adolescents break out of the cocoon of family life and reach for a far bigger world. In this chapter we've suggested a middle road for parents and teens, a road that encourages teenagers to remain appropriately bound to family with ties of Christian love while simultaneously being prepared to move beyond their family into God's bigger world.

Opening Prayer

Open with prayer, asking each member of the group to thank God for a good memory he or she has of childhood family life.

Scripture Readings

Ruth 1: What can we learn from this chapter about family ties and family loyalty?

Luke 15:11-32: If this parable of the lost son portrays our life as children in God's family, what lessons might we as Christian parents learn about life in our own families?

Philippians 2:4: Remember this verse as a caution against self-centeredness.

For Discussion

What Would You Do?

1. Invite members of your group to find a middle-road response to the situations listed below. Perhaps you could do this in small groups, reporting your responses to the larger group later on.

    a. Jonathan, the teenager introduced at the beginning of this chapter, is your son. He has just informed you that he refuses to show up for grandmother's dinner and birthday celebration.

    b. Your daughter Brenda is fifteen years old. As a ninth grader, she would like to go to the school basketball game but would much rather sit with you than with her classmates.

    c. Your daughter Megan signs up for helping in the church nursery on the Sunday her nephew Timmy is being baptized. You think she feels jealous because of all the attention you've been giving your first grandson.

d. Your son Brandon reports that he'd rather stay home and work this summer while the rest of the family goes on the annual two-week family camping trip.

e. Your seventeen-year-old daughter, Suzanne, tells you she's planning to be with her boyfriend's family on Christmas Eve. That's the time your family has always exchanged gifts.

f. Your fifteen-year-old adopted son, Jeff, tells you he won't be able to go out to eat with the family tonight to celebrate his sister's tenth birthday. He claims he has to work. He has often accused you of spoiling her because she's your natural-born child.

The Importance of Family Traditions

2. Family traditions are built upon pleasant patterns of family life. Each family has the opportunity to carve out its own unique traditions. Children should be encouraged to see themselves as key players in this process. Their family is creating a legend . . . perpetuating traditions that will hold a treasured place in their memory banks for the rest of their lives. These traditions are often the cement that holds families together.

Here are some treasured yet simple family traditions worth considering:

- "Our family goes out for breakfast every Saturday morning. One of the kids chooses the restaurant each week."
- "Dad always sits around the kitchen table with us for snacks before we hit the sack at night."
- "We go camping every Fourth of July weekend."
- "Every Monday night we have leftovers for supper."
- "We call Grandpa and Grandma every Sunday afternoon. We all get to talk with them for a few minutes."
- "We watch our family's favorite TV program together every Tuesday evening."
- "Each of us kids received an autographed leather-bound Bible from the folks after completing sixth grade."

Invite members of the group to share pleasant memories and family traditions that have grown out of their experiences at family mealtimes, on family vacations, and while celebrating a special family event.

Ask members of the group to identify some traditions they hope to build for their families.

3. This chapter suggests that children who have been neglected or abused will have little family loyalty as teenagers. Ponder the impact of neglect and abuse on the future of family life in our society. Perhaps the group can identify some subtle forms of neglect and abuse that may sometimes sneak into busy, successful families like ours.

4. Discuss the impact that the following experiences might have on a teenager's attitude toward his or her family:
   - Heavy conflict between parents.
   - Repeated separations and reconciliations of parents.
   - Divorce of parents.
   - A teenager's mother remarries. The stepfather moves in, along with two of his children by a previous marriage.
   - A teenager's father dies in an auto accident.

5. "Adopted children are less likely to demonstrate family loyalty than natural-born children. Adopted adolescents experience heightened anxiety about their roots and, consequently, about their identity. Parental enforcement of rules and punishments often leads them to feel unloved and unwanted. It should not surprise us, then, that adopted children often resent family ties that bind."

   Agree or disagree with the above quote, defending your viewpoint.

6. Loving parents of adolescents often make a special effort to embrace their adolescents' friends as friends of the family. They encourage their children to bring their friends over to their home. Ample space, generous snacks, and clear acceptance are always offered. What do you think about this strategy for strengthening family ties? Does it work for you?

Closing

Close the session by sharing thoughts about the kinds of messages we send our children about our own commitments to family ties. What do we do to stay in touch with our parents and other members of our extended family? In the decisions we make about our time, money, and recreational activities, what are we saying about how important our children are to us?

Pray silently for God's presence in our families. You may want to conclude by singing "Blest Be the Tie that Binds" (*Psalter Hymnal* 315; *Rejoice in the Lord* 407, 408).

FIVE

THE QUEST TO BE BLEST

Teens aren't really very different from us. They need to know they are loved, just as we do. In fact, all God's children need constant reminders that they are accepted and affirmed by God and by God's other children. When people know they are loved, they have positive self-esteem. When people question that love, doubting their worthiness, their self-esteem is strained and sometimes even shattered. During the stormy transitions and challenges of adolescence, teenagers crave assurance that we love them.

To love others is to bless them, to pronounce a benediction of favor and assure them of our acceptance. It's not always easy to bless people who bother us . . . and it just could be that at times we're bothered by our teenagers. For example,

- our son disregards curfew rules.
- your daughter refuses to clean her room.
- your son shows up with the weirdest haircut you've ever seen.
- your daughter tells you she thinks she's pregnant.
- your son comes home drunk. You can smell the alcohol a mile away.

But . . . grace loves anyway! And adolescents need that *anyway* of grace.

The *anyway* of unconditional love is seldom an easy order for parents. Teens at risk are often trying hard to get our attention by making a statement or asking a profoundly crucial question.

The statement might go something like this: "I think my parents resent having to put up with me. They would probably be happier if I weren't around to mess up their lives. I'm just being the kind of kid they tell me I am. So what's new?"

The questions might go something like this: "Do they really notice that I'm here? Do they care enough to keep in touch? Do they love me enough to confront me on these problems I'm creating? Do they really care?"

My hunch is that in some sense *most* teens are at risk. Most of them test their parents' promise to love them. And most teens are in real conflict: On the one hand, they are moving toward independence, which makes them want to distance themselves from their parents; on the other hand, they seek a relationship marked by mutuality (and even intimacy!) with parents. They need to know that their parents love them *anyway!* Positive self-esteem is the product of that kind of unconditional love.

Parents of adolescents also experience conflict during this transition time. To unconditionally love teenagers who may think, feel, and act in ways we dislike often seems impossible. I believe our greatest struggles and challenges as parents come during the crucial years when our children wade through adolescence. All our prayers, hopes, and dreams for our kids are put on the line . . . and often we must let go of our dreams while hanging on to our teens! They are on a quest to be blest. And God sends us on a mission of mercy. Grace loves anyway!

An Inferior Interior

We all begin life with some feelings of inferiority. Our earliest days of self-awareness lead us to the conclusion that most people seem bigger, stronger, and wiser than we are. And that's absolutely true! Life becomes a process of discovering our name and our place in this post-womb world of challenges and threats.

Children who are noticed, hugged, respected, nurtured, challenged, corrected, and listened to move beyond feelings of inadequacy to a growing sense of self-confidence. Children who perceive that they are considered worthy and lovable by those closest to them readily believe in God's love for them as well. Any lingering questions about their worth are offset—but never completely removed—by daily demonstrations of affirming love.

Adolescents address these questions, which lurk in their "inferior interior," with newfound zeal. And it may be that we unknowingly send subtle messages to teens that sometimes fuel their renewed journey into self-criticism. The basic issue has to do with our ability to love unconditionally. Do we love the person we want our teenagers to *become*? Or do we love the teenagers who live in our homes today—the teens who keep a messy room, who forget to shower, who yell at their younger brothers and sisters, who flunk algebra, and who come home drunk on a peaceful Sunday evening.

Teens are quick to interpret our rejection of their misdeeds as our rejection of them as persons. Take the story of sixteen-year-old Ray as an example.

"I hate his projects!" Ray told me, as he reviewed his feelings about life at home. This teenager was red-faced and angry when describing the great amounts of time and money his father invested in building his utility shed, remodeling the porch, and even constructing a swimming pool for the family. Ray admitted that he was doing poorly at school, staying away from home overnight with his friends (without parental approval), and becoming a fairly heavy drinker. He said that what really got him so mad (and led him to continue these behaviors) was that whenever he got into trouble, his father would just ground him and assign him work on these home-improvement projects as punishment. "I know I'm just one big disappointment to my dad. He never has time to talk with me. Ever since I gave up the idea of going to college to become a lawyer like him, he's lost interest in me," Ray said.

Ray is not his real name, but the above paragraph is not fiction. I worked with this young man for quite some time, helping him deal with his temper flare-ups and rage attacks. Ray viewed parental reprimands and penalties as rejections. He felt that he would never be able to meet his parents' expectations for him. He yearned for their blessing and acceptance but became increasingly convinced that he was unworthy of their love. In response, he started demonstrating just how bad he really was.

The Hug Lines of Life

A hugging family is usually a healthy, happy family. Hugs symbolize closeness and acceptance. Ideally teenagers do not stop hugging members of the family on their thirteenth birthday. Instead they form a longer "hug line." As teens move to certify their right to life beyond the bounds of family life, they need to be hugged by others as well.

Acceptance by others becomes a central concern for most thirteen- and fourteen-year-old adolescents, and entry into high school is often a time of heightened anxiety. A number of factors may help us understand why this is so.

1. Younger teens fear being teased and ridiculed by more mature students.

2. Earlier friendship patterns are often weakened as ninth graders find their place in their new high school setting.

3. With varying timetables for the onset of puberty, teens devote a great deal of attention to their own physical development. Teens dread the thought of being "late bloomers." Shower-room comparisons after gym class can either strengthen or shatter a teen's sense of self-esteem.

4. Maturing mental processes invite teens to question and critique parental values and customs. This process generates the fear of losing parental love.

5. A teen's basic authority is experience. In their frantic quest to be blest, teens often assume that what peers do is what they want to do, simply because that's what's being done by the friends they admire.

6. Heightened body changes may lead to chemical imbalances, which at times contribute to feelings of unworthiness and depression. Messages of rejection then take on added weight.

7. Competitive themes often complicate a teenager's quest for acceptance by peers. The same teen who works hard to get the highest grade in algebra, or to make first chair in the trumpet section of the school band, or to be one of the starting five on the basketball team, may also worry about being resented by his or her nearest rivals.

8. Conflicting values between teens' parents and peers may leave them confused and anxious. Parents may push for academic excellence, while peers may ridicule a dedicated student. Teens often feel pressured to make difficult choices.

9. Teens seek constant assurance that they are accepted by members of the opposite sex. Teens who feel unnoticed and unwanted often feel utterly crushed in spirit.

Even a casual review of that list reminds us that our teens' quest to be blest will not always be readily achieved. Teens seek hugs from their peers, but they may not always get them in return. Often peers, sought out as a new source of support, instead cause a great deal of pain for teens.

Why is this so often true? A subtle theme of self-centeredness undergirds much adolescent thinking and living. The teen who readily conforms to peer pressure often does so to feel accepted and loved by others. The underlying drive for most teens is simply the need to know they are accepted. This does not mean adolescents are unilaterally selfish and unloving. I do believe, however, that it is important for parents to recognize that an adolescent's primary developmental task is to come to terms with his or her own identity. This means that teens will generally place greater priority on having their own needs met than on meeting the needs of others.

Examples of the hazards of our teens' hug lines abound.

Your daughter Melissa is really looking forward to Friday night. After the game, her best friend, Jennie, will be coming over to spend the night. They're planning to order a pizza and watch a video. But Thursday evening Jennie calls to tell Melissa that she's not coming on Friday, since a guy just called to invite her to the game.

Your son Derek is thrilled to be on the basketball team, and he's even getting to play once in a while now. He complains to you, though, about how Greg, the star player, will never feed him the ball if it's at all possible to take the shot himself. Greg's working on setting a school record for scoring the most points in one season.

Jennie and Greg both need to be accepted and affirmed—but so do Melissa and Derek. Situations like these can be very painful for teens who crave evidence of acceptance. The decisions made by Jennie and Greg underscore the power of this underlying adolescent drive to gain recognition and approval—and the hazards of that drive for other teens, like Melissa and Derek. The same teen hug line can be both healthy and hazardous!

The Search for Security

We all work with hunches, and teens are no exception. In fact, we are all being bombarded with a hunch, a theory, about how to be accepted and loved by others. The message comes to us from the media and goes something like this: *You will surely be accepted if you meet the world's criteria of appearance, acquisition, and achievement.* In other words, if you're good-looking, if you own the right things, and if you can out-perform your nearest rivals, you'll be a success.

This scheme, so widely accepted in our society, effectively cancels Christ's call to love as he loves us, and it gives adolescents (as well as adults) the wrong approach to gaining acceptance by others. The focus of this scheme is really *cruelty* rather than *compassion.*

Think of how many teens are deeply hurt because of unkind remarks peers make about physical features that cannot be changed.

Think of the subtle (but sometimes blatant!) ways that kids are made to feel inferior and unwanted simply because they cannot afford designer jeans, the right kind of tennis shoes, or their own personal car. Teens from well-to-do families who intentionally exclude lower-income classmates from their parties flagrantly violate Christ's call to kindness and caring.

Think of the poverty of "peak performance" as a valid norm for acceptance. As Christians, we should realize it's not *being the best* but rather *doing one's best* that is important for every one of God's children. Parents, pastors, teachers, and coaches should be as concerned for the psychological, social, emotional, and spiritual well-being of the 995 teenagers sitting on the bleachers as they are for the five basketball stars playing the game. There can be only one best grade on an exam in each classroom, one first-chair violinist in each orchestra, and one valedictorian in each graduating class. But no teen should ever receive the message that "we accept the best and disregard the rest."

Even our grading theories deserve critical review. The only acceptable norm for grades, as our Lord presents it in the parable of the talents (Matt. 25:14-30), is to determine whether we do *our best* with the talents God gives us. There should be no winners and losers in our homes, classrooms, and churches.

What Can Parents Do?

As our teens move beyond the relative predictability of the love messages they receive from family members to the less-certain world of peer acceptance, we need to keep hugging them. Why? Because they undoubtedly need our hugs more during this stage of their lives than ever before!

What can we do to assure them of our love?

• *We should love them for who they are, not for what they do.*

And we should tell them so. Our focus as parents is on *being* rather than on *doing*. Persons like Joni Eareckson and Dave Dravecky remind us that our worth is not tied to our performance but to our presence. Joni lost her ability to move about freely because of a diving accident. Dave Dravecky's career as an ace pitcher was ended when he lost his throwing arm to cancer. But these people are whole persons, full of grace and truth! They deserve to be loved and accepted for who they are, not for what they can do.

For our teens, this also means they can do something wrong without thinking of themselves as being bad persons. Conditional love scrutinizes performance before embracing the person. Unconditional love always accepts, always forgives, always affirms . . . whether we consider another person's behavior to be acceptable or unacceptable. Our teens need to know that we believe this and that we pledge to put it into practice.

- *We should reject the heresy of "the gifted child."*

I believe that good parents and well-meaning educators can get sucked into the trap of victimizing their kids by buying this heresy. If the parents of four sons, Matthew, Mark, Luke, and John, constantly refer to Luke as a gifted child, they have made a clearly heretical statement about Matthew, Mark, and John. When good teachers speak of Lisa as a gifted child, they are making two judgments: Lisa is gifted, and her classmates aren't. And that's heresy!

I believe we parents have to watch our language. Using the label "gifted" can kill the spirit of our teens. Children who never hear themselves referred to as gifted may begin to believe that God really loves a few smart people—the ones who were given special gifts. These "deprived" kids are intelligent enough to conclude that if God had truly loved them, they would have been given special gifts too. Because of that, I believe the label "gifted" grieves God as well. God decorates each and every person with gifts and grants each of us the power to exercise them for the Creator's glory. *In God's book, every teen is a gifted person!* We should believe it—and our teens should know we believe it to be true for them. Tell them often!

- *We should houseclean our hearts.*

Remember Ray, the teenager who hated his dad's projects? Ray was convinced that he would be cherished and loved by his father only *if* he successfully completed high school, college, and law school.

Fathers and mothers need to own up to the private and sometimes public dreams they hold for each of their children. They should do so honestly and carefully, because these dreams play a powerful role in forming the attitudes we take toward our children. For example, a father who regrets having dropped out of high school may literally demand that his son graduate from college. This may turn out well, but it may also backfire. Pressures around school performance will mount, and Dad's love for his son will then be based on the condition of academic success.

Some teenagers feel tremendous pressure from parents to excel in sports. A parent's need to feel very proud of a successful teen athlete may say more about his or her personal feelings of inadequacy than about the teen's interest and abilities in sports. Teen jocks often stand as a parent's trophy. We should remember that our children are not a second chance for us to accomplish the things we failed to do in our own lives.

- *We should pledge to keep our teens honest.*

As teens dabble with the idea that self-centeredness will carry the day, we should courageously assist them in destroying that myth. Teens may test us by wanting to be indulged. They often resent limits. They may abhor the suggestion that sharing is "in." They may expect frequent use of the car, free gas, meals fixed to order (on their personal timetable!), and daily room service as well. Keep them honest. As members of a family, they are obliged to carry their share of the load. Car privileges are not to be simply assumed. Fuel is not free. Mother does not do all the dishes.

We all face frustrations in life, some of which cannot be magically removed. There are times when we are all forced to change our plans. That's life. Mature persons have learned the lesson of delayed gratification. Just because we want something does not automatically mean we can have it. "Later" can be a loving answer to a teen's sometimes stringent demands.

• Empathize with their struggles.

Parents of teens should remember that their struggles are very real. They do agonize with the conflicting pressures to compete while still caring for others. They swing back and forth between the need for intimate relationships with parents and for the mutuality of open relationships with peers. They feel the need to be dependent, while at times claiming independence. Mood swings bring them to pinnacles of optimism but also down into the pit of despair. Teens can criticize you at breakfast and bury you with compliments at suppertime. They need to know that we empathize with their struggles. Tell them so often.

• Don't buy their theory on toys!

We do know and believe that what they own and the quality of clothes they wear will never guarantee them the acceptance they seek. No teenager wants to be considered a nerd. And we want them to feel accepted by their friends. But we should help them to look beyond the labels, the brand-names, and the need for toys. Toys are fun, but we don't need the latest in styles of clothes, jet skis, and sports cars to be blest by others! Let them know you are asking the Lord to free you and them from the temptations of materialism.

• Tell each of your children they are beautiful!

Redefine beauty in terms of character rather than physical appearance. Beautiful persons give and receive love. Think of beauty as a fruit of the Spirit: Beautiful is to be blessed and to bless others.

• Focus on compliments rather than on criticisms.

It's surprising how often we can zero in on the few inappropriate things others do rather than on the many wonderful things they've done in the course of a typical day. Constructive criticism, of course, can be helpful, if it is offered in love. But nagging, repeated public criticism and put-downs can do considerable damage to a teenager's sometimes fragile ego.

Teens are on a quest to be blest. That's just another way of saying they need to know they are loved. As they search beyond their family for indications of affirmation and acceptance, continue to assure them of your loyal love. Hugs at home build positive self-esteem, which equips them for responsible Christian living.

Suggestions for Group Session

Getting Started

In this chapter we've underscored the point that teenagers need to know they are loved. Christian parents are called to foster positive self-esteem in all their children.

Our emphasis on self-esteem is based not on pop psychology but on biblical principles. Gordon L. Bordewyk wrote in the October/November 1990 issue of *Christian Home and School,*

> We clearly err if we uncritically embrace self-esteem as a panacea for all our woes or shortcomings in the classroom or at home. But we also fail in our responsibilities as parents and teachers if we do not instill in our kids the confidence that they belong to God and that they are valuable members of his kingdom.

Our assurances of love for our teenagers can become our Lord's benediction!

Scripture Passages

Genesis 37:1-5: Jacob favored Joseph over his other sons. Reflect on the implications of this favoritism for family life.

Luke 14:12-14: What do we learn about mature love in this passage?

Matthew 25:14-30: What lessons can the parable of the talents teach us about holding realistic expectations for our teenagers?

Opening Prayer

Each group member should report something positive about each of his or her children. Afterward share prayers of support for the families represented.

For Discussion
Is Positive Self-Esteem Biblical?

1. Evaluate and react to the following two quotes. What implications does each of them have for the way we deal with our teens?

   Some books seem too eager to have people feel good about themselves. The Bible certainly contains the good news that self-esteem folks love to announce, but they seem to forget that in Scripture you first have to hear some very bad news.

   Wayne Joosse, "The Christian's Self-Image: Issues and Implications"; Occasional Papers from Calvin College, vol. 5, no. 1; Grand Rapids, MI; Jan. 1987; p. 34

   I do not deny that according to the Scriptures we are all by nature depraved or sinful . . . however, many of us tend to look only at our depravity and not at our renewal. We have been writing our continuing sinfulness in capital letters, and our newness in Christ in small letters. We believe in our depravity so strongly we think we have to practice it, while we hardly dare to believe in our newness.

   Anthony Hoekema, The Christian Looks at Himself; Grand Rapids, MI: Eerdmans; p. 18

   a. Are we tempted to downplay the "bad news" of sin with our teenagers? Are we overemphasizing positive self-esteem in our homes, churches, and schools?

   b. How can we help teens to be honest about their sin and their need of forgiveness without threatening their sense of self-worth?

2. Use these quotes to assist you in reflecting on the impact of parent pressure and peer pressure on an adolescent's sense of self-esteem. Which quote is most helpful to you as a parent? Why?

   These teenagers do not seem to believe anything terribly different from what their elders believe; they simply believe it while floating untied to anything outside their high school world. No one refers to an adult authority (except, sometimes, a parent), to a book, a magazine article, a TV news show. Even Christian kids seem to refer to the Bible only as an afterthought. Not only do they lack perspective, they have no idea they lack it. Their only authority is experience.

   —Tim Stafford, review of Teenagers Themselves in Christianity Today, Oct. 19, 1989, p. 84

Adolescence can be a trying time—particularly for the teenage boy. He is exultantly proud of his newfound sense of masculinity, but his body, alas, remains an embarrassment. Where are those flauntable biceps and triceps? . . . Scrawny youngsters, some only 13, eagerly pay between $50 and $400 to black-market dealers for a six-to-thirteen-week cycle of pills and injectables that could turn them into Hulk Hogans.

—Anastasia Toufexis, *"Shortcut to the Rambo Look,"*
Time, *Jan. 30, 1989, p. 78*

In America's increasingly competitive society, the bad report card—once fodder for Norman Rockwell and Leave it to Beaver—is no longer a laughing matter. More and more social workers, educators, and police are recognizing that report-card time can trigger a torrent of emotional and physical child abuse.

—Anastasia Toufexis, *"Report Cards Can Hurt You,"*
Time, *May 1, 1989; p. 75*

Try to create an atmosphere in the home in which the children accept each other. The children should be encouraged to appreciate each other's talents and gifts, and to cheer each other along when they learn new skills or make other kinds of progress.

—Anthony Hoekema, The Christian Looks at Himself, *p. 116*

Some Helpful Hints for Christian Parents

3. Anthony Hoekema includes a helpful section in *The Christian Looks at Himself* in which he offers suggestions about how parents can help their children develop a positive image of themselves (pp. 112-123). Reflect on ways to translate these recommendations into action steps with your teenagers.

   • Christian parents should communicate to their children the fact that they belong to God.

   • Parents should also communicate to their children the fact that they are totally accepted by father and mother.

   • Parents should try to create an atmosphere in the home in which the children accept each other. (See Hoekema quotation above.)

   • Parents should also handle disciplinary problems in such a way as not to damage a child's positive self-image.

67

- Parents, further, should encourage their children to become more and more independent as they grow older.
- Parents should build up a child's self-esteem by indirect means, such as using a caring tone of voice and offering appropriate praise.

Final Considerations

4. Reflect on some of your own childhood experiences. How was self-esteem cultivated or threatened in your family of origin?

5. What's happening in your family, church, and school that encourages the development of positive self-esteem in our teenagers? Identify some things we could do better to provide more loving support to our teenagers.

6. Are we too competitive in the world of academics, sports, music, and income? Should adolescents be warned about the dangers inherent in a competitive spirit? Support your hunches.

Closing

Close by imagining what might change in your family if you were to frequently look your teenagers straight in the eye and promise to love them for who they are rather than for what they do. Ask for God's help in showing love and respect to your teens.

SIX

PAINT THEM A RAINBOW

An artist did a great job of painting a beautiful rainbow on the wall of the quiet room at Pine Rest Christian Hospital. This room is often used by our adolescent patients when they're feeling discouraged and depressed. They may go there by themselves to think, to meditate, and to reflect on the issues they're dealing with. For some, the rainbow means nothing, since all they see is the darkness of their depression. But for many, the rainbow on the wall is like a small candle in a very dark room. It becomes a ray of hope, even when life seems quite hopeless.

God wants all of his children to remember the rainbow—not only Noah and his family but you and me as well. Christian parents should be in the business of painting rainbows on the walls of their children's quiet rooms.

Sara saw God's rainbow, but it took her a long time to get it into focus. She told me about her broken home, her feelings of unworthiness after being sexually abused by an older brother and by her mother's live-in boyfriend, and her belief that none of her peers liked her at all. She was lonely, depressed, and suicidal. She was also blind to God's rainbow.

But God's rainbow came into focus for Sara during the course of her treatment and counseling. She began to feel accepted, respected, and loved—especially after she met a young man who loved her for who she was rather than for what she could do for him. She wrote this poem in order to share her excitement at discovering God's rainbow:

THE RAINBOW
A baby of innocence, a baby of joy,
Misused she was, used as a toy.
The child rebelling, the child knew pain.
Why they were cruel, she couldn't explain.
In adolescence, the tears would flow.
She was blinded from the sight of God's rainbow.
He created it for her, to show her love.
To get in the right direction required a shove.
As a woman, she found happiness.
It washed away insecurity and loneliness.
She had found love, in a simple man.
To grow and heal, she began.
In her boyfriend's arms, her face aglow,
She now knows she's loved.
She sees God's rainbow!

I believe God is calling us to be agents of hope for our teenagers. And the way to equip teens with hope is to surround them with appropriate expressions of love. In this chapter we will look at some of the tough issues that arise in our dealings with adolescents . . . issues such as substance abuse, sexual acting out, and fights over church activities. In the face of heavy conflict, communication breakdowns, and major losses, how can we still paint rainbows for our teens?

The Need for a Creed

One of the most loving things parents can do for their children is offer them firm moral principles, values, and guidelines that work when "the rubber hits the road." In my contacts with troubled adolescents, it never ceases to amaze me that so many young people have not been favored with that kind of guidance.

You may recall reading of an incident that occurred several years ago to a pilot in Florida. One day he planned to fly his vintage biplane and had it sitting at the beginning of a runway. He spun the propeller until the engine started, and then he kicked the blocks away from the front wheels. As he turned around to climb into the cockpit, he was shocked to discover that his plane was taking off without him! It circled around the airstrip once and then headed out over the Atlantic Ocean. He never saw his plane again.

Sending teenagers into the young adult world of choices and decisions without a clear set of moral guidelines is like watching a plane take off without a pilot. Unharnessed energy is always destructive—

whether it's a firecracker, a car on an icy road, or a person living without the Lord.

I believe we should be very direct in telling our teens that God's Word does offer a life plan that works. The Creator knows what it takes for our lives to come together in rich and meaningful ways. As a coach needs a playbook, a conductor needs a score, a builder needs blueprints, and a pilot needs a flight plan and maps, so all of God's children need guidance about how to live as members of God's family. Parents are remiss and unloving if they fail to instruct their children in the ways of the Lord.

Paul reminds us to "take captive every thought to make it obedient to Christ" (2 Cor. 10:5). Many teenagers have stated very clearly to me that they feel cheated because their parents seldom, if ever, take the time to help them develop a road map for their journey through adolescence. Children and teenagers feel cherished and loved if we invest our energy in offering them a solid foundation upon which to build their lives.

Today's teens are confronted with a wide range of values that directly contradict the teachings of Scripture and the Christian church. Our attitudes about issues such as smoking, use of alcohol and drugs, honesty, competition, materialism, sexual acting out, and racism are constantly impacted by messages sent via TV, movies, entertainment heroes, sports figures, and even peers. In subtle ways, Satan permeates these messages with themes of self-centeredness.

Our teenagers need and deserve to be instructed on how to discern the Lord's will in all these complex areas of their lives. Without that kind of guidance and nurture, their lives will be impoverished. Teens who know that Christ is the pilot of their plane are well equipped to see God's rainbow.

Our teens need a creed just as much as a plane needs a pilot!

Drinking and Drugs

One form of adolescent behavior that causes parents a great deal of concern is their teens' use of alcohol and drugs. Because experimental use seems acceptable to most teenagers, adolescent abstainers are a rare species. Even preadolescents feel pressured to drink beer and to smoke pot! Which one of these kids reminds you of your teenagers?

- *Todd*—He does well at school and already knows where he wants to go to college. He dropped football this year because he needed more study time. He helped to organize the local chapter of SADD (Students Against Drunk Driving) at his school. He reports having no interest whatsoever in drinking and thinks "potheads" are stupid.

- *Tam*—She admitted taking her first drink as an eighth grader but apologized for doing so. She seems to be fairly well motivated now as an eleventh grader and plans to go to college (if she doesn't get married first!). She dates frequently and stays out as late as she can every Friday and Saturday evening. She insists that she and her friends don't drink beer at their parties, but recently she came home smelling like a brewery. You decided to ground her for a week. You're really worried about her.

- *Tim*—School has been a bad word for Tim since third grade. You really wonder if he'll make it through twelfth grade, especially now that he's just been suspended for one week. He was caught drinking behind school again this noon—his third offense. He's also come home drunk several times. You're really not too surprised, since he always challenges your rules and protests all your penalties. He moves among a group of negative peers who would all drop out of school this week if their parents approved.

Our teenagers live in a world that encourages adolescents to link casual use of alcohol and drugs with being adult. Statistics indicate that close to 90 percent of high school students nationwide have at least occasionally used alcohol. In a survey of sixteen- to eighteen-year-old Christian young people, however, conducted by the Calvin College Social Research Center in Grand Rapids, Michigan, only 54 percent of the respondents admitted to having drunk beer, wine, or other alcoholic beverages at least once during the past year. Twenty-three percent of that number drank one or more times per month.

Parents should be alert to patterns of alcohol and drug use among teenagers. We should remember that an unwary teen can quickly move beyond the stage of initial experimental drinking to a pattern of regular use and then on to abuse and chemical dependency. Abusers often give indications of "clusters" of deviant behavior, which might include lying, stealing, cheating, aggressive acting out, declining interest in school and church activities, and overall defiance of parental and family values.

Parents who see their teens moving in this direction can often recognize the shift away from *pro-social behavior* to *at-risk behaviors*. Drinking and drugs are strongly correlated with smoking, sexual acting out, disregard of vehicle safety codes, and depression.

Statistics are impersonal. But how about your kids? Parents of drinking teenagers ask compelling questions about why their sons and daughters are choosing to drink. That's a question researchers continue to wrestle with. Yet while they may not be able to offer accurate reasons for any one teen's decision to drink, they have identified attitudes that most users hold in common. For example, teenage drinkers often place low value on academic achievement and have little expectation of being successful in school. They place great value on independence, and they expect it as well. Users show diminishing interest in religion and moral values, prefer peer to parental orientation, and are more tolerant of transgressions than their non-drinking peers.

Human behavior is functional. In other words, we all make decisions as part of our strategy to survive and to succeed. Teenagers decide to drink because it fills a function they consider useful for them at this point in their lives. For example,

- Drinking can function as a symbol of status transformation. To drink is to shift from feeling less mature to feeling more mature, from being thought of as a young adolescent to being admired as an adult.

- Drinking guarantees teens solidarity and acceptance by peers.

- Drinking can be a way to cope with feelings of frustration. Self-medication often assists a person who has been trained to deny his or her feelings. Getting high or drunk is simply more pleasant for someone who fears feeling lonely, sad, or angry.

- Drinking can be an effective medication against expected failures.

- Drinking can be a statement of angry protest, defiance, and rebellion against family, church, and community values.

Adults are often forced to reckon with the fact that drinking and drug use are very powerful weapons in a teenager's arsenal. Teens can accurately predict that if they come home drunk or stoned, their parents will become angry, lose their tempers, become deeply anxious, and be filled with shame. These reactions give rebellious teens feelings of power and control which they may be seeking at this time. So drinking is often nothing less than effective breakaway behavior.

Christian parents are called to respond to adolescent drinking and drug use with compassion and candor. Compassion leads us to maintain communication as a two-way street. Love empowers us to listen and to learn from drinking teens how their behavior fits into their world of values and friendships at this time. But candor leads us also to confront inappropriate and unacceptable behavior head-on. Drunkenness is unbiblical, and we should say so. Drinking is illegal for minors, and we should say so. Use of drugs is a clear violation of the law, and we should say so. Drinking without parental approval and supervision violates family rules, and we should say so.

Our teens should know of our concern that they honor Christ as Lord of their lives. They should know we are concerned about the damage alcohol and drugs can cause to their body, mind, and spirit. They should know our concern is motivated by our love for them.

Let me say a word about our words as well. The way we communicate our values, beliefs, and expectations in situations like these is crucial! In the heat of anger and conflict, poorly chosen words can bring relationships between parents and teens to the breaking point. Accusations, yelling, name-calling, threats of extended punishments, and even physical scuffles can do irreparable damage.

In these difficult encounters Christian parents must seek the Spirit's moderating presence and guidance. Our goal should not be to control our teens' behavior so much as to assure them of God's deep care and love for them. We want them to acknowledge the Lord as the pilot of their plane, even as they make decisions about their use of alcohol and drugs.

A final note here regarding the messages we send by our own attitudes and actions: Parents must honestly reckon with their own drinking patterns as they seek to understand their teens' decision to drink. Parents who need the self-medication of a martini in order to survive family conflict, who allay their anxieties by downing a bottle of wine with every evening dinner, who enjoy weekly parties where liquor flows freely, and who unwittingly provide teens open access to the family liquor cabinet have no basis for blaming their children for following their example. The sheer hypocrisy of a parent who lectures a teenager on the dangers of drinking while holding a Whiskey Sour in his hand will drive children away from their parents and the values they verbally endorse. Parents also need a creed!

Condoms in the Closet

Starting sex education when our children are teens is like lecturing someone on how to operate their parachute after they've jumped out of the plane. Since sexuality is so basic to one's sense of personal identity, discussions of sex should begin in early childhood. Parents should encourage their sons to accept their masculinity and their daughters to accept their femininity as a beautiful gift. Appropriate expressions of one's sexuality and the cultivation of warm relationships with others should be consistently discussed and modeled in Christian homes.

74

Adolescence has been described as a time of "chemical explosions." The onset of puberty is marked by dramatic changes in children's body chemistry. The appearance of secondary sex characteristics indicates that the sex drive is moving onto center stage. Teenagers need to prove to themselves and to their peers that they are no longer children.

Heightened concern over their own development and appearance often leads teens to prove they can function physically as adults. Teens crave attention from peers and often seek concrete evidence of their acceptance by friends of the opposite sex. They live in the NOW of excitement, pleasure, and stimulation. Talk about commitment and long-term consequences is unusual.

Sensitive parents understand these trends as indicators of healthy development and will respond with discretion to their teenager's growing fascination with the human anatomy and human reproduction. Parents accidental discovery of pornographic material in their son's closet need not be the occasion for guilt-inducing lectures but rather the opportunity for further discussions about his growing interest in sex.

There is a significant difference, of course, between a teenager's growing interest in sex and his or her participation in sexually inappropriate behaviors. The parents who found the magazine will undoubtedly want to foster open communication with their son on the subject of sexual development. However, if they also find a package of condoms in his closet, their determination to talk will skyrocket! National studies indicate that by age fifteen and a half at least 50 percent of boys have experienced sexual intercourse and that by age sixteen more than half of all girls have gone "all the way." By age nineteen, seven out of ten females and eight out of ten boys are no longer virgins.

Cliff is a sixteen-year-old boy of slight build, marked by clear academic abilities. He's not a jock by any stretch of the imagination. He feels socially inadequate and prefers isolation to the risks of seeking acceptance by peers . . . at least most peers. Recently he confessed to his school counselor that he has become intimately involved with an equally shy female classmate. He had given no thought to birth control until his girlfriend expressed the fear that she might be pregnant. The counselor advised Cliff to share his concerns with his parents. He responded with visible horror and shock. He says his parents would be absolutely devastated.

Maria is seventeen years old, the second of two girls in what appears to be a happy family. However, beneath the veneer of happiness is a lot of pain. Maria is adopted, and she feels that her adoptive parents clearly favor her older sister Rachel, their natural-

born daughter. Rachel excels at school, helps with household chores, and talks constantly about college. Maria loves sports and boys. During the past year she has become sexually active. In fact, rumor has it that she's an "easy take" for any willing male at school. Her parents recently confronted her on their suspicions, and she acknowledged her promiscuity without regrets.

Christian parents are sometimes shocked to discover that their teenagers are involved in sexual acting out. You place utmost value on virginity before marriage, and they laugh you off as hopelessly outdated. You focus on purity, and they celebrate passion. You tell them to be Christian in their dating, and they say they would rather not let religion interfere with their relationships.

Adults know better than adolescents that sex is serious business! Unbridled intimacy, heavy petting, and intercourse carry long-term consequences that teenagers naively or willfully overlook. Impulsive intimacy and serial sexual encounters leave partners feeling dirty, guilty, and unloved . . . later.

But Christian parents are also called to look behind the behavior to the motives. Cliff's parents need to help him discover realistic reasons for building more positive self-esteem. They need to help him address his feelings of inadequacy and to encourage him to cultivate appropriate friendships with male and female peers. Maria's parents also need to work with her on identity issues related to her feelings as an adopted daughter. They need to encourage Maria and her sister, Rachel, to openly review the quality of their relationship. Maria's sexual acting out must be seen as the messenger of deeper, underlying issues requiring significant attention.

Christian parents should be proactive in offering sex education as an ongoing feature of healthy family life. Children who learn to distinguish between acquaintances, companions, friendships, and intimate relationships are better equipped to assess their own relationships as adolescents. They will be able to think about sexual intimacy as an indicator of the commitment Christians make when they marry. They will be encouraged to distinguish between appropriate and inappropriate sexual behaviors. They will have a creed for courtship that labels some activities as acceptable and some as clearly unacceptable.

Christian parents will encourage positive friendships and dating practices for their adolescents. They will not load excessive guilt on early adolescents who explore their growing sexuality. Intimacy will be appropriately modeled at home. Inappropriate sexual attitudes and actions will be addressed with candor and compassion, but forgiveness and new beginnings will be the order of the day. God's teenage children need lots of rainbows!

When Faith Feels Forced

It was encouraging to learn from the youth survey mentioned earlier that 85 percent of the Christian teenagers interviewed desire to live a life that is pleasing to God. Nine out of ten attend church services every Sunday, and seven of those nine say they go because it is important to them. That's impressive and encouraging!

But that doesn't mean Sundays are always smooth sailing for the typical Christian family. Probably most families experience growing tension about levels of participation in church life. Many teens come to resent feeling pressured to attend church services, church school, or catechism classes, as well as other youth group functions. While, as committed parents, we seek to offer Christian nurture, instruction, and training in the Christian faith "to the utmost of [our] power" (remember those promises you made when your teens were baptized fifteen years ago?), we don't want our teens to feel as though we're forcing our faith on them. Teens do not become disciples of Christ because parents demand it!

Cindy begins every Sunday morning angry these days. She's sixteen and the oldest of three children. Her family is known as one of the pillar families in the church: not even a blizzard will keep them from getting to church on Sunday.

Cindy started rebelling against religion soon after she signed up for a gymnastics class on Wednesday evenings. She'd been training in gymnastics for only a few weeks when the church began a mid-week high school youth fellowship group on Wednesday nights. Her parents told her that being a responsible member of the church family demanded that she drop her gymnastics class.

Cindy exploded and started reciting all the restrictions the church was placing on her life—including her parents' insistence that she be home by 10:00 on Saturday evenings so that she can be wide awake for church services on Sunday mornings . . . .

I suspect that each of us could write our own little story about family faith fights. It may begin with your kids wanting to sit with their friends in the balcony rather than with the family. Then come the questions:

- "Why do I have to go to church twice every Sunday?"
- "Why do I have to go to church with you on Sundays?"
- "Why should I have to show up for youth group? None of the other kids in my class go."
- "Why don't you just let me make up my own mind about morals and religion?"

77

Faith fights are always difficult and painful, because we want our children and young people to embrace the One who embraces them. We want our kids to be devout and committed Christians. We live with the vision that they will join us as loyal, active members of the church.

Mature Christians, however, know that the Christian faith cannot be forced. Kings, church leaders, and parents have tried to do that over the centuries without success. History proves that plastic piety withers in the heat of real-life struggles. So we nurture, train, and instruct our children in the faith, always praying that our efforts will be energized by the Spirit's power. We pray that our teens will realize that religion is not our package but God's promise to love and cherish them always. We pray that they will celebrate membership not just in our family but in God's family as well. While not forcing faith, we strongly endorse radical surrender to the One who died for us.

But it's important to remember that the teens who challenge our expectations are the very ones who are seeking ways to establish their own identities as emerging adults. These teens are often less concerned about pleasing parents than peers. If 90 percent of their friends attend a megachurch on Sunday evenings, your demand that they join you because you value worshiping together as a family will place them at a painful crossroad.

I believe it's appropriate for parents to allow growing space for teens to clarify their own values, to establish their own priorities, and to chart their personal courses in response to the promised love of Christ for them. Perhaps Cindy's parents could have worked out a compromise with her on her Wednesday-night commitments . . . suggesting that she attend her gymnastics class for the first semester, then attend the church function for the second semester. In addition, a caring parent might join Cindy as advocate, approaching the pastor to suggest alternative scheduling of church programs for teens like Cindy and her friends.

We're Not Building Birds' Nests

When baby birds are strong enough to fly, they leave the nest for good. But parents committed to strong family life are not building birds' nests! We're in the business of incorporating our children into a family embrace that will last a lifetime. Family ties should not be seen as an entanglement to be shunned but rather as a relationship to be cherished.

I recently learned of a Dutch tradition in which newlyweds enter their new home through a certain door and then never use that door again until the day they die. This tradition symbolizes the fact that family ties are absolutely dependable. Commitment to live together in love is the cement that keeps family members close. Teens need more than a bird's nest that they will leave behind forever. They need family ties that guarantee them an enduring relationship of love. Where love binds families together, relationships will be rich and rewarding. Family rituals and reunions will be cherished. Teenagers will feel kinship and membership. They will believe that they have a name and a place in their clan. They will know and love their roots, and they will always know they belong!

Healthy families are not perfect but forgiven. Open communication, honest dialogue, and willing confession keep parents and teens close together. Rigid parents often find themselves sidetracked on control issues. Conflict rather than cooperation then prevails. Firm faith blended with a flexible attitude toward the sometimes unpredictable actions of teens brings daily reminders of Christ's compassion and love.

And that's the deepest message we want our teens to hear. In an address to youth workers a few years ago, Rick Van Pelt suggested the following guideline for parents. He proposed that parents give their teens the *gift of time*:

T—Teaching our values and beliefs

I—Involvement in one another's world

M—Modeling the messages we speak

E—Encouragement

Teens will respond in love to parents who demonstrate the love this involves. Through your *gift of time* they will see God's rainbow!

Suggestions for Group Session

Getting Started

In this final chapter we've taken a look at samples of family conflict related to teen substance abuse, sexual acting out, and arguments about church involvement. Parents of teens are often confused over how to handle situations like these. Do we tighten the rules and penalties? Do we minimize the problems in the hope that things will be better next week? Do we simply grant teens full freedom of choice?

As parents, we struggle with the tension between wanting to maintain a friendly relationship with our teens and the need to "hang tough" with our beliefs and values. If we place more emphasis on being accepted by our kids than on providing them with dependable guidelines for growth, they will feel betrayed. We can most effectively paint them a rainbow by being mature models of the Christian faith, offering them consistent guidance, understanding, and love.

Scriptures

Romans 15:1-7: Paul underscores some Christian virtues in this passage that offer guidance to families experiencing conflict.

1 Corinthians 6:18-20: This passage reminds us of the contrast between sexuality as an occasion for sin or as part of our praise to God.

Opening Prayer

Offer sentence prayers, each of you thanking God for the good things happening in your families and asking the Lord for help in dealing with specific issues and problems that may be making family life painful.

For Discussion
When Problems Hit Home

1. We love our teens deeply and believe the Lord loves them too. God embraces them as members of the covenant family. That's what makes it so shocking and painful when Christian parents' worst fears are sometimes realized and a major behavioral problem shatters their dreams of a happy family life.

   What should you do when your family seems to be falling apart? As a group, identify two or three crises your families have or may encounter and together come up with a plan for healing the family.

Drinking and Drugs

2. Review the three stories in chapter six:

   Todd—the abstainer

   Tam—the experimenter

   Tim—the abuser

   What causes teens to fall into any one of these three tracks? Describe the kinds of friends you think Todd, Tam, and Tim probably hang around with.

3. What do you think the Bible teaches about the use of alcohol? Review 1 Timothy 5:23, but also look at passages like Ephesians 4:27 and 5:18.

4. Many parents actively encourage their teens to participate in non-alcohol parties, etc. Share suggestions on what you could be doing to "make a difference" for teens in your town.

5. Identify alcohol and drug information and prevention programs available for teens in your community. Do you support efforts like these? What more could churches be doing to help teens involved in substance abuse?

6. If your teenager comes home drunk, what should you do? Is it ever appropriate to kick him or her out of your home for failing to abide by your rules? Explain.

Sexual Acting Out

7. Share your childhood experiences on sex education. Where did you learn about sexuality and the differences between appropriate and inappropriate sexual behaviors?

8. What have you been doing to teach a biblical perspective on sexuality and relationships to your children and teens?

9. What would you do if you accidently discovered birth control pills in your daughter's drawer or condoms in your son's closet?

10. If you were Maria's parents, what would you do to assure her of your love while emphasizing your concerns about her sexual activity?

11. If your daughter became pregnant as an unmarried high school student, how would you respond? What support would you hope to receive as a family from your church and school community?

Struggles Over Sunday

12. What are Sundays like at your home? How do you handle your teens' resistance to your expectations that they join you in church activities?

13. What are the ingredients of family life for teens who do not resist but rather endorse their parents' religious values?

14. Should teens have not only a voice but also a choice when it comes to decisions about attendance at worship and youth group activities? If so, at what age?

15. How do you encourage your teens to make profession of their faith without having them feel you're inappropriately pressuring them?

16. Evaluate this approach: *"As long as you live under our roof, you will join us at church . . . twice every Sunday!"*

Closing

As you close your final session together, you may want to consider some of the following quotes and the ideas they offer for building healthy relationships within the family. Then close with prayer, asking for God's wisdom and patience as you parent your teenage children. Thank God for covenant promises that assure you, even in troubled times, that your teens are brothers and sisters of Christ, members of God's family.

Are We In Tune with Teen's Issues?

In the January 30, 1991, issue of *The Christian Century*, Daniel R. Heischman summarizes the findings of a recent Girl Scout Survey, a nationwide review of the moral and spiritual perspectives of some five thousand children and adolescents in grades four through twelve. He writes,

> *What adults perceive to be crucial issues facing young people are not necessarily deemed crucial by the youths themselves. Young people worry most about fulfilling adult expectations (80 percent about obeying parents, 78 percent about getting good grades, 69 percent about preparing for the future, 62 percent about earning money), instead of what adults routinely perceive to be the big crises in growing up—sex, substance abuse, peer pressure. Perhaps we adults are the ones fascinated with sex, drugs and rock 'n' roll, while youth carry an adultlike burden of worries.*
>
> —p. 110

A Teen's View on Premarital Sex

Matt Ramsey, an eighteen-year-old from St. Peters, Missouri, addressed the subject "Why I've decided to wait" in the February 1991 issue of *Breakaway*, a teen magazine published by *Focus on the Family:*

> *God created sex as a gift. To have sex before marriage is to spoil the gift. It's kind of like Christmas. The presents are under the tree and your parents leave the house. You secretly unwrap the gifts to see what's inside. But when Christmas Day comes and you open the gift at the right time, it's not as special. It's no longer the surprise you waited for. I don't want to spoil such a special gift as sex, especially since God has specifically told me to wait.*

Parents Held in High Regard by Teens?

In the Summer/Fall 1990 special edition of *Newsweek* magazine, featuring today's teenagers, David Gelman summarizes research attempting to measure the depth of teen's respect for parental values:

> *The researchers found "far more congruence than conflict" between the views of parents and their teenage children. We much more frequently hear teenagers preface comments to their peers with "my mom says" than with any attributions to heroes of the youth culture. . . .*
>
> *—p. 15*

A Teen Speaks Out Against "Teen-Bashing"

In that same issue of *Newsweek*, Brad Wackerlin, a high school senior, writes that he is not a druggie, a delinquent, or a dropout. He challenges adults to rethink their habit of "teen-bashing." He concludes his article with these words:

> *My only goal in writing this article is to point out the "bum rap" today's teenager faces. I feel the stereotypical teen is, in fact, a minority. The true majority are the teenagers who, day in and day out, prepare themselves for the future and work at becoming responsible adults. Our time is coming. Soon we will be the adults passing judgment on the teenagers of tomorrow. Hopefully, by then, we will have realized that support and encouragement have a far more positive effect on teenagers than does "bashing" them.*
>
> *—p. 22*

Controlling Others Is Sick!

That's the title of the article Rev. Jim R. Kok wrote in *The Banner* on September 10, 1990. Do you agree with his advice for parents?

> *Each of us is strongly tempted to control others, especially our children. Usually we would like them to live out an agenda we think best. Occasionally our designs are sensible and appear correct. But our plan always has one weakness—it is ours, not theirs.*
>
> *As young people mature, parents walk a narrow path between discipline and control. Sometimes we slide over the line, urging, judging, or conniving and manipulating to get our children to live out a script we have written. What we really need to do is to free them to write their own.*
>
> *—p. 11*

SUGGESTED READING LIST

Balswick, Jack O. and Judith K. *The Family*. Grand Rapids, MI: Baker, 1989.

Benson, Peter, Dorothy Williams, Arthur Johnson. *The Quicksilver Years*. San Francisco: Harper & Row, 1987.

Benson, Peter L. *The Troubled Journey: A Portrait of 6th-12th Grade Youth*. Minneapolis: A RespecTeen Resource, Search Institute, 1990.

Buntman, Peter H. and Eleanor M. Saris. *How to Live with Your Teenager*. New York: Ballentine Books, 1979.

Campbell, Ross. *How to Really Love Your Teenager*. Wheaton IL: Victor Books, 1981.

Coles, Robert. *The Spiritual Life of Children*. Boston: Houghton Mifflin, 1990.

Curran, Dolores. *Stress and the Healthy Family*. Minneapolis: Winston Press, 1985.

Curran, Dolores. *Traits of a Healthy Family*. San Francisco: Harper & Row, 1983.

Dobson, James C. *The Strong-Willed Child*. Wheaton, Illinois: Tyndale, 1978.

Elkind, David. *All Grown Up & No Place to Go*. Reading, MA: Addison-Wesley, 1984.

Hoekema, Anthony A. *The Christian Looks at Himself*. Grand Rapids, MI: Eerdmans, 1975.

Joosse, Wayne. "The Christian's Self-Image: Issues and Implications." *Occasional Papers from Calvin College*, vol. 5, no. 1; Grand Rapids, MI: Jan. 1987.

Kesler, Jay, ed. *Parents & Teenagers*. Wheaton, IL: Victor Books, 1984.

King, Paul. *Sex, Drugs & Rock 'n' Roll*. Bellevue, WA: Professional Counselor Books, 1988.

McDowell, Josh. *What I Wish My Parents Knew About My Sexuality*. San Bernardino, CA: Here's Life Publishers, 1987.

Montgomery, Mary. *Home Is Where the Start Is*. Minneapolis: Winston Press, 1985.

Parsons, Richard D. *Adolescents in Turmoil, Parents Under Stress: A Pastoral Ministry Primer*. New York: Paulist Press, 1987.

Paul, Jordan and Margaret. *From Conflict to Caring*. Minneapolis: CompCare Publishers, 1989.

Powell, Douglas H. *Teenagers: When to Worry and What to Do*. New York: Doubleday, 1987.

Sell, Charles M. *Family Ministry*. Grand Rapids, MI: Zondervan, 1981.

Shelton, Charles M. *Adolescent Spirituality*. New York: Crossroad, 1989.

Strommen, Merton P. *Five Cries of Youth*. New York: Harper & Row, 1974.

Strommen, Merton P. and Irene. *Five Cries of Parents*. New York: Harper & Row, 1985.

Sawyer, Kieran. *Sex and the Teenager: Choices and Decisions*. Notre Dame, IN: Ave Maria Press, 1990. (Leader's Guide also available.)

Shedd, Charlie. *You Can Be a Great Parent*. Waco, TX: Word Books, 1970 (Key-Word first edition—1982).

Wangerin, Walter, Jr. *As for Me and My House*. Nashville: Thomas Nelson, 1987.

Magazine Suggestions

Christian Home & School, CSI, Grand Rapids, MI.

Focus on the Family, Pomona, CA.